PrayerFoundation Evangelical Lay Monks ™

# Prayer as a Total Lifestyle
## Learning from the Greatest Lives of Prayer

## by S.G. Preston

*"True prayer is a way of life..."*

-Billy Graham
1991

———

*"The end of every monk and the
perfection of his heart direct him to
constant and uninterrupted
perseverance in prayer;*

*and as much as human frailty allows,
it strives after an unchanging
and continual tranquility of mind
and perpetual purity."*

-Desert Father Abba Isaac
c. 420 A.D.

2nd Edition

*PrayerFoundation Press* ™
Vancouver, WA 98687 U.S.A.

There are a few references to fasting in this book. Certain people should never fast: pregnant women, the sick, those with diabetes and certain other medical conditions. Before fasting, check with your Physician first, to learn if this is something you can safely do.

———

ISBN-13: 978-09995307-1-9

Preston, S.G., 1951-

PrayerFoundation Evangelical Lay Monks ™
*Prayer as a Total Lifestyle*
*Learning from the Greatest Lives of Prayer*

1. Prayer.  2. Celtic Christianity.  3. New Monasticism.
4. Christian History.  5. Evangelicals.  6. Threefold Daily Prayers.

————

Print Edition and eBook Edition
created for publication by:
*PrayerFoundation Press* ™

————

Published by:

*PrayerFoundation Press* ™
Vancouver, WA 98687
Email: monks@prayerfoundation.org

Books by S.G. Preston:

*PrayerFoundation Evangelical Lay Monks* ™
Series:

*Prayer as a Total Lifestyle*
*Prayer as a Celtic Lay Monk*
*Answers to Prayer*

These books have been written to inspire and motivate you to draw nearer to God in prayer.

Filled with a selection of the best quotations from some of *The Greatest Lives of Prayer*, they can also be used as a Daily Devotional.

Their extensive Indexes (in the Print Versions) make them useful as Reference Works.

They have been written in an easily understood style to make them suitable as *"prayer encouragement"* gifts for friends, relatives, and young people.

Dedicated to:

My partner in life, ministry, and prayer…
my beautiful and loving wife,
Linda.

*"Evening, and morning, and at noon;
I will pray and call out loud,
and He shall hear my voice."*

-Psalm 55:17

———

*"Rejoice always.
Pray without ceasing.
In everything give thanks.*

*For this is the will of God
in Christ Jesus concerning you."*

-1 Thessalonians 5:16-18

v

Our Mission:

*"To Promote Prayer Among All Christians
and Proclaim Christ to the World."*

Scripture Basis:

*"But we will devote ourselves continually to prayer, and to the
ministry of the word."* -Acts 6:4

Learning from the Greatest Lives of Prayer:

*"When asked, 'What is more important: prayer or reading the
Bible?' I ask, 'What is more important: breathing in or breathing
out?'"* -Charles Spurgeon

# Contents:

# 3. *A Life of "Prayer Without Ceasing"*

# 4. *Great Lives of Prayer in History*

# 5. *Spurgeon, Taylor, Müller*

# 6. *The Original New Monasticism*

## Prayer and Evangelism:

*"When Billy Graham was asked about the most important steps in preparing for an evangelistic outreach, he always answered that there were three things that mattered most:*

*prayer, prayer, and prayer.*

-Cliff Barrows (1923-2016)
(Music and Program Director for the
*Billy Graham Evangelistic Association*)

―――

*"Precede all your labors with earnest, diligent prayer. Do not rest on the number of tracts you have given because a million tracts may not lead to the conversion of a single soul. Yet, a blessing beyond calculation may result from a single tract.*

*Expect everything to come from the blessing of the Lord and nothing at all from your own exertions."*

-George Müller (1805-1898)

―――

*"Every convert is the result of the Holy Spirit's pleading in answer to the prayers of some believer."*

-From the book, *The Kneeling Christian* by Anonymous

―――

*"Prayer is your way, often the only way, to water the harvest. By prayer you can bring the Holy Spirit's blessing on any Gospel effort anywhere in the world."*

-Wesley L. Duewel (1916-2016) Missionary to India

\* \* \*

S.G. Preston

## *What Other Christians Say About Us*

**I am with the *Billy Graham Evangelistic Association* and we're working on a children's project** in which we are seeking permission to use a photo of George Mueller...I found his picture on your site. How (do we) obtain permission to use it? Blessings,

*-Jack W. Munday (Ministry Manager, Billy Graham Evangelistic Association; Asheville, North Carolina)*

Thank you for your prompt and helpful response!!! Blessings,

*-Jack W. Munday (Ministry Manager, Billy Graham Evangelistic Association; Asheville, North Carolina)*

---

(10/7/02)

**My son Bill answered your recent e-mail about having a film on St. Columba.** As he indicated we have talked about this for years with our good friend Norman Stone, a Director living in Scotland.

I have been overseas but Bill sent me a copy of your email and I was fascinated to learn about your community and would love to know more about your order, its discipline, where you are located, when founded, etc.

Thanks for anything you may provide.

*-Ken Curtis (Founder: Gateway Films/Vision Video; Christian History Institute, Christian History Magazine)*

It was so interesting to learn of your community and the details of your devotion to the Lord. We find ourselves thrust into the middle of daily battle in the media worlds of Christian communication which only causes us to pause to thank God from

11

time to time for those he has raised up to keep the incense of prayer stoked and burning before his presence continually…

So as and when our little ministries should ever come to your mind, we would be so grateful if you would intercede before the Lord on our behalf…

Again, we rejoice to know you are there. Your brother in Christ,

*-Ken Curtis (Founder: Gateway Films/Vision Video; Christian History Institute, Christian History Magazine)*

---

**I've been blessed visiting your website a number of times in the recent weeks. I particularly like the book and film recommendations.** Being of Irish heritage, I'm intrigued by your emphasis on Celtic Christianity. This is an area I would love to spend more time studying. I also want to thank you for including *Wycliffe Bible Translators*…

I am a translation advisor serving with SIL in Papua New Guinea, translating the N.T. and some O.T. materials into the Bariai language. Praise God, he has blessed this work and helped us greatly in these past 16 years! Many blessings in Christ for the New Year.

*-Steve G. (Missionary Translation Advisor, SIL / Wycliffe Bible Translators; Papua New Guinea)*

---

**I'm looking for some photographs of J. Hudson Taylor to be used on a book cover for *Discovery House Publishers* in Grand Rapids, Michigan.** Do you know who owns the original photographs or rights to them? Please help! Thank you!

*-John M. Lucas (Discovery House Publishers; Grand Rapids, Michigan)*

S.G. Preston

---

**As a Franciscan Friar, I found your website to be very interesting.** I am excited by your ministry; I am especially interested in hearing of communities such as yours which clearly demonstrate how much we all share in common. May the Lord continue to bless you and your worthwhile ministry. Peace and all good!

*-Brother Albert, OFM (Order of Friars Minor)*

---

**I have been a monastic in the Russian Orthodox Church for 34 years** and can certainly recommend your approach as a spiritually sane way of living monastically.

…you are offering a type of monastic experience that seems to be able to be experienced in both a remote and an urban setting.

I most certainly will pray for your Order, and if I were in the world would seek a place in it.

May God Bless your work, I am your unworthy servant,

*-Hieromonk Kyrill (Holy Nativity of the Theotokos Hermitage, Illinois)*

---

**I was happy to see the article on MAF (*Mission Aviation Fellowship*)** seeking educators for the children of their missionaries.

*-Lay Monk Denise (Missionary in Japan)*

---

**I am an ordained minister and a full time student at *Liberty University*.** I have been to your Site many times. It has really grown and I like the direction.

I have little time for things outside of school, but I do hope to be able to fit more things into my day, including these prayers (on your website): *Daily Prayer: Praying the Hours*.

I look forward to praying with you all.

-*Brent* (*Texas*)

---

**We are actively involved in a Celtic church planting project here.** Please add me to your subscription list.

-*Eric D. Benson, D.Min.* (*Highland Faith Fellowship*: *a Celtic Southern Baptist Community of Faith, West Virginia*)

---

**Loved your website. It inspired me to take Friday to chant all 150 Psalms. What a blessing!** We use the *St. Dunstan's Plainsong Psalter* and the 1928 *Book of Common Prayer* for our choral/chanted Morning Prayer and Evensong services.

-*Ian G.* (*Lay Leader of St. Vincent of Lerins Anglican Church, Oregon*)

---

**I am a minister with the *Christian & Missionary Alliance* Church. For many years now I have been searching for an evangelical monastic community.** I am excited to read about your community. I am 39 years old. My other job is as a psychotherapist in a local drug rehabilitation facility.

14

The monastic spirituality has been a real source of inspiration and growth in my spiritual journey. I hope to start something similar in the Philippines someday. Previously, I have lived in the United States for a year, helping an evangelical ministry set up its own therapeutic community in San Francisco.

At the moment I am doing my doctoral program in clinical psychology and writing my dissertation in psychotherapy which I hope to finish this year, Lord willing.

*-Ruel (Minister, Christian & Missionary Alliance, Philippines)*

---

**I am so thankful I found your website! It is...finding like-minded believers.** I have been strongly drawn to *Lectio Divina.* Just wanted to say thank you -- I am planning on humbly submitting my application to become a part of your Order. May God continue to bless and prosper your ministry.

*-Pastor Mike (Methodist Minister)*

---

**I find your website very informational, and refer to it every day. Visit daily.** At times there are things I would like to share with my friends, some are on *Facebook,* and others are not. Would find it very helpful if a link was placed on every page to share your message with others. Pray for me as I attempt to finish up my Ph.D. in Theology. God bless your ministry. Practicing the *Great Commission* in my life daily.

*-W. Michael N. (Seminary Student; Toledo, Ohio)*

---

**I am a pastor from Pakistan. I was very happy to view your website.** I am married and my wife is Gurya, we have 3 daughters and one son. I am very happy to watch your website and I have been blessed through your site. I pray for you and your family and your ministry.

First, I was a Sunday school teacher, and youth preacher, and outreach leader; now I am a pastor. God has enabled me to establish Church in different villages working with many tribes and peoples in different parts of Pakistan. Yours in Him,

*-Rev. Javed (Pakistan)*

---

**This is a wonderful Site! Level-headed, too. You even have the good Dr. Luther as one of your favorite monks! I am a Lutheran pastor serving in the Philippines,** and I am, to say the least, impressed by your website.

It is a refreshing refuge from an often troubling world. Thank you for encouraging me to pray...I have been so indolent in my prayers.

Luther said that true monasticism is being faithful and excelling in the vocation to which God has called you. If it is to be a carpenter, then be a good carpenter, and so on.

And it seems that you have excelled in the vocation to which God has called you. You are, by far, the most excellent monks I have ever met.

*"For the faith being ever one and the same, neither does one who is able at great length to discourse regarding it, make any addition to it; nor does one who can say but little, diminish it."*

Irenaeus was certainly right about that. In seminary we were admonished time and time again never to play with the Creeds for the sake of *"creative worship."*

16

The Creeds were written for a specific purpose; i.e., to clarify and proclaim the Christian faith, to refute the heretics, and to provide a spiritual reference point to which one goes back in times when doubt assails him.

Reading Irenaeus again was refreshing.

The *PrayerFoundation*™ is indeed an oasis in the desert that is the *"net."* I am praying for you. In the name and fellowship of our Lord Christ,

*-Lutheran Pastor (Cagayan De Oro, Philippines)*

(Author's Note: Irenaeus, *Against Heresies,* 1.10)

---

**I am a recent graduate of *Moody Bible Institute*, and am descended from the families in Ireland that once served in the abbeys before Rome's intervention.** I'm also attending *Trinity Evangelical Divinity School* in the fall.

I am Irish (and my mother is a Scot). I am very familiar with the Celtic Church from my family, as well as my studies.

It was good to know that both my schools were at the top of your list. In Christ,

*-John M. (Seminary Student; Chicago, Illinois)*

---

**Our publishing house is preparing a book about European monuments on the *UNESCO World Heritage List* and we cannot find photos regarding *Skellig Michael*.**

Would it be possible for you to advise us of a photographer who offers pictures of this site of the quality suitable for printing? Thank you,

*-Lenka Moravcová (Otto Publishing House; Prague, Czech Republic)*

---

**So happy to have found you. I am a member of the *Canada Yearly Meeting (Quakers)*.** I have been *"a monk at heart"* for many years, trying to maintain my own discipline. I am 75 years of age. Joining you will make it so much easier. Yours in Christ,

*-Gerrit (Quaker; British Columbia, Canada)*

---

**By nature I enjoy people, and as a *Baptist pastor*, I know that activity and noise is usually preferable to silence. It has been a rich and rewarding time over these many years.** Then, a year ago, I stumbled across the idea of *New Monasticism.*

This morning as I researched articles on the "net," imagine my joy to find a prayer movement for evangelicals devoted to the core areas of my interest. I immediately forwarded your link to my prayer group of pastors who meet every Monday afternoon. Together we are *Christian Reformed, Baptist, Congregational, Anglican, Independent Christian Reformed Evangelical,* and *Apostolic Pentecostal!*

So, please add me to your email list. My thanks for calling us back to our common roots. Every joy from *Nova Scotia, Canada* which has as its Scottish roots the motto: *100,000 Welcomes!*

*-Pastor Quincy C. (Baptist; Nova Scotia, Canada)*

---

**I read with interest your observations about the early forms of Celtic stone crosses in Ireland and Scotland.** I appreciate and praise God for your website. We are praying at fixed hours in a prayer garden behind our house that used to be a 24 foot in-ground swimming pool.

Now in our late 70's, we are finally retiring from pastoral ministry at the end of this calendar year, while remaining active in the church apart from professional pastoral or clerical concerns.

In the words of our denomination's (*Church of the Brethren*) 300th anniversary slogan, we are yours: *"Surrendered to God, Transformed in Christ and Empowered by the Spirit."*

*-Jim and Letha McK. (Pastor, Church of the Brethren; Virginia)*

---

**We are producing a new religious education programme for Anglican primary schools in Ireland** and have the story of Amy Carmichael within one of the lessons. We would really like a photograph to accompany this. (Request concerning obtaining photograph; and any applicable copyright permission). This is a non-profit production, with 5,000 books printed and sold to schools at cost. If you would like any further information, I would be happy to oblige.

*-Jennifer B. (Church of Ireland Board of Education; Dublin, Ireland)*

---

**Myself and my wife Mele are Christian missionaries to the *Kingdom of Tonga*,** and we have a video book and CD/DVD lending library for our ministry to the people here. I happened to see your site when I was searching for *Pilgrim's Progress,* which we hope to soon buy and use to show the people how to walk with the Lord Jesus (evangelism, discipleship, etc.) Thank you for your *Prayer Ministry* and thank the Lord for everything He is doing all over the world, even here in Tonga!! When we cry out to Him – He will answer. Amen. Love in Christ,

*-James and Mele (Missionaries in the Kingdom of Tonga)*

---

**I am a priest in the *Independent Anglican Communion* and live in Northern Ireland.** I have been to your website many times and have found it very stimulating. I am retired and am at present constructing an oratory in the garden for prayer. Is it possible for a priest to join you in your ministry?

*-Fr. Douglas (Anglican Priest, Northern Ireland)*

---

**This is Rev. Jon. We have met several times. We visited your monastery in Vancouver, Washington, and you visited us...** I now teach a Spiritual Disciplines Class at *Horizon Christian High School.* I have showed my students your website and we are all fascinated by the idea of a Born-Again Monk.

*-Rev. Jon (Horizon Christian High School, Oregon)*

P.S.: This is the students of *Horizon Christian High!!!!!!!!!!!!* Please come to our class and tell us about yourself, we would very much appreciate it. You are the coolest monk we have ever heard of. We are truly interested in what you have to say. Please bring your shields and robes!! They are tight. Thanks, bye!

---

**I learned from your website about the *Celtic Christian* services at the *Gospel Community Rivermont* Church in Lynchburg, Virginia.** My parents live near there, so we all went to the *Celtic Christian Christmas Eve* service this year. It was very beautiful. Thank you,

*-Heather W. (North Carolina)*

S.G. Preston

---

I have been to *New Skete* on the east coast...overall *their example, and sites like yours, show that monastic worship and aspiration are not something to be put on a pedestal...* I am sure that others who struggle with this battle for the Gospel will find your approach clean and insightful.

The way is simple, direct and possible. I hope that your community is successful in maintaining high integrity to the Gospel... Yours,

*-Jacob* (Staffmember for the website of the *Greek Orthodox Archdiocese of America*)

---

**Subscribe.**

*-Marty Cardinal Malkin* (*St. Philip Neri ArchDiocese*)

---

**Dear Lay Monk Preston & Lay Monk Linda, Greetings in the name of our Risen Lord! We are writing you on behalf of *The Communion of Evangelical Episcopal Churches.*** We have kept up with you and the ministry over the years and have been greatly blessed by your love for Christ and the Church. We are especially blessed by the way you are encouraging people to know the Lord and grow in his Grace and Love.

We should have written a long time ago to tell you we appreciate you including the CEEC in your *History of Protestant Monasticism*. We have many people who have continued to pursue an evangelical monastic life. This week beginning October 21st, 2009 the CEEC Bishops are meeting in Synod and we thought it would be nice if we could read a letter of greeting and prayer to the Synod, from *The Prayer Foundation*.

This would also give us a nice way of exposing more people to your website. Other fellow "monastics" have been kind to do so, we have included one example from Ray Simpson from Lindisfarne. In Christ,

*-The Bishops of the CEEC*

---

**I have accepted Christ as my Lord and Savior, this date.**
...I accepted Christ as My Savior while visiting the *PrayerFoundation* ™ website.

*-Merle (Florida)*

---

**I accepted the Lord Jesus Christ as my Savior on your website, and it continues to be an inspiration to me.** In addition I tell anyone who will listen about your good works.

My attraction to your Site was the simple beauty and clarity of the message, and it continues to be the same today. Your Brother in Christ,

*-Doug (Colorado)*

---

**I am truly glad to have found your website. I have a great desire to follow Jesus Christ. Today I have accepted Him in my heart and asked forgiveness of my sins.** Now, today, I feel the strength to give my life and my heart to Christ. Thank you for inspiring me (to be saved).

I am a small farmer, with a wife, and wonderful son and daughter. I live in rural Northeast Thailand. There are no Christians here (I know, hard to believe). I guess I could try to be the first. I have been here for five years now, and life is very different than Vermont, U.S.A.

I will try to seek out fellowship in the big city of Bangkok. I go there every once in a while, but it is a six hour drive away. I do feel like a monk in my heart (one with lots of solitude). I will continue with God's help to grow in Christ.

I believe I am here in the boonies for a purpose. I pray that my wife will come to accept Jesus Christ (I guess this could be a prayer request!), and that I may be a strong example for my children.

I pray I can be strong in faith as I am surrounded by those that worship spirits (life in the village is quite medieval in flavor). Thank you again. Your brother in Christ,

*-David (Thailand)*

## Aidan of Lindisfarne (c. 590-651 A.D.)
## Celtic Christian Monk That Led Northern England to Christ

*"He cultivated peace and love, purity and humility. He was above anger and greed, and despised pride and conceit. He set himself to keep and teach the laws of God, and was diligent in study and in prayer...I greatly admire all these things about Aidan."*

*"He was one to traverse both town and country on foot, never on horseback, unless compelled by some urgent necessity; and wherever on his way he saw any, either rich or poor, he invited them, if unbelievers, to embrace the Faith; or if they were believers, to strengthen them in the Faith, and to stir them up by words and actions to good works.*

*"This (the reading of scriptures and psalms, and meditation upon holy truths) was the daily employment of himself and all that were with him, wherever they went. If it happened, which was seldom, that he was invited to eat with the king, he went with one or two clerks, and after eating a small meal, hurried to leave with them, either to read or write."*

*"He never gave money to the powerful men of the world, but only food, if he happened to entertain them; and on the contrary, whatever gifts of money he received from the rich, he either distributed them, as has been said, for the use of the poor, or bestowed them in ransoming those that had been wrongfully sold as slaves.*

*In addition, he afterwards made many of those that he had ransomed his disciples, and after having taught and instructed them, advanced them to the order of the priesthood."*

-The Venerable Bede (672/673-735 A.D.)
*Ecclesiastical History of the English Nation* (Book III, Chap. 5)

\* \* \*

# *A Very Short Introduction*

In 1999, after a trip to ancient monastic sites in Ireland, and a visit to St. Francis' hilltop town of Asissi in Italy, my wife Linda and I Founded the very first *Evangelical Monastic Order* on the Internet; the *only* one for the next four years.

I had been "Googling" *Born Again Protestant Monks* for months, and no organizations ever came up. The new website that we started: *The Prayer Foundation:™ Born Again Protestant Monks* at: *www.prayerfoundation.org* would be the first to do so.

Our original Website grew to over 1,300 webpages of what we called:

*"The Best of Prayer Teaching and Resources from All Christian Communions and Eras."*

Early on it went viral, receiving up to 2.4 million page downloads per month; nearly 30 million each year; 600 million over the past 20 years. Yes, that's *over half a billion* total page-downloads – no one was more surprised by this than us!

Unfortunately, due to unresolvable technical issues, we have been unable to update our original website since 2014. Our new website that we created in 2020: *PrayerFoundation Lay Monks ™* at: *www.prayerfoundation.net* contains many of our original Site's best 100 webpages, but in a much updated magazine-style format.

Our ministry has been tremendously influenced, guided, and inspired by C.S. Lewis' book, *Mere Christianity*. We describe our *PrayerFoundation™* ministry as a *"Mere Christianity"* ministry, summed up by this famous C.S. Lewis quote:

*"Ever since I became a Christian*
*I have thought that the best,*
*perhaps the only, service I could do*
*for my unbelieving neighbors*

*was to explain and defend the belief*
*that has been common*
*to nearly all Christians*
*at all times."*

Our Christian Ministry is International and Interdenominational; during the past twenty years we have been joined by over two-thousand Registered volunteers (Prayer Warriors and Lay Monks) from 47 countries. One out of every seven of the Lay Monks are either Pastors, Youth Pastors, Missionaries, Bible College or Seminary students, and this has been the case from the beginning.

We also established from the beginning, an all-volunteer ministry, with no one, including the Founders, receiving any compensation. For us, it is indeed a labor of love, our offering of ourselves to God. It was also our decision from the start, not to do any mailings or other high-pressured appeals for funds, but just to pray for them.

By Interdenominational, we mean that all Lay Monks remain in their own individual Churches or Denominations (whatever type of Protestants, or Roman Catholics, or Eastern Orthodox).

Members also remain in their own homes, with their own families, in their own jobs or careers; and yes, we allow men *and women*, single *or married*, to become Lay Monks with our *Knights of Prayer Lay Monastic Order!* ™

Please pray for us. May God richly bless you as you serve Him!

*Pax et bonum! Peace and all goodness!*
(This was St. Francis' motto, greeting and blessing.)

Yours in Christ,

S.G. Preston
(Lay Monk Preston)
Vancouver, Washington
St. Patrick's Day, 2018

S.G. Preston

## St. Augustine (354-480 A.D.) Writing About Prayer:

*"What can be more excellent than prayer; what is more profitable to our life; what sweeter to our souls; what more sublime, in the course of our whole life, than the practice of prayer!"*

———

*"Trust the past to God's mercy the present to God's love, and the future to God's providence."*

———

*"You don't love in your enemies what they are, but what you would have them become by your prayers."*

———

*"Even the straws under my knees shout to distract me from prayer."*

———

*"Do what you can and pray for what you cannot yet do."*

———

*"I never have any difficulty believing in miracles, since I experienced the miracle of a change in my own heart."*

———

*"Prayer is the key that opens heaven; the favors we ask descend upon us the very instant our prayers ascend to God."*

———

*Your desire is your prayers; and if your desire is without ceasing, your prayer will also be without ceasing."*

\* \* \*

# *Answers to Prayer*
### *PrayerFoundation™ 24-Hr. Prayerchain*

**Apr. 30, 2001 - Urgent Prayer Request:**

Hello. My name is Caroline. My father is going to have open-heart surgery this Thursday. Would you please say a prayer for him? I just cannot imagine life without him. He has been the greatest dad that anyone could ever ask for.

We've been through some tough times together. My mother left us back in 1991. It was a hard time. Us kids would rebel and take our anger out on him for her leaving. I myself always ran away when I just couldn't take the pressure anymore.

But my dad never gave up on us. He continued to work to put us through Catholic High School. I am now 27 years old. I just need extra prayers for him to make it through this ordeal. I really appreciate your help. Thank you so much.

**Answer to Prayer - May 2, 2001 (Two days later.)**

Dear Lay Monk Preston & Family,

I want to thank everyone from the bottom of my heart for your gracious prayers. My dad is doing fine now. He went to the hospital today to get a catheterization done to clear up his arteries. Now the doctors said that he does not need the open-heart surgery tomorrow!!

THANK GOD!!!!! He is a miracle worker!!! Today was a total blessing. Now my dad has to just recover from today's minor surgery. I'm sure that'll go well, too.

Love, -*Caroline*

---

(From the book: *Answers to Prayer* by S.G. Preston)

28

# 1: *Born Again Protestant Monks*

## 1.1 Assisi: Where St. Francis Walked

*"Most High, all powerful,*
*all-good Lord,*
*all praise is Yours,*
*all glory, honor and blessings.*

*To You alone, Most High,*
*do they belong;*
*no mortal lips are worthy*
*to pronounce Your Name."*

-St. Francis of Assisi (1181/82-1226 A.D.)
From his song, *Canticle of Brother Sun*

**Assisi, Italy**

In December of 1998, Linda and I visited the small hilltop town of Assisi. The train trip from Rome required an entire day of traveling through the Italian countryside.

At the base of the mountain, we transferred to a bus taking us to the end of the line: a parking area just below the medieval town. After climbing a long series of steep steps, we arrived at the town proper.

No vehicles are allowed on the ancient streets. From the top of the mountain, the view was breathtakingly beautiful.

Far below was the vast panorama of undeveloped rural Italy: fields, vineyards, and farmhouses, extending as far as the eye can see. At this time of year there were almost no tourists.

Small remnants of snow, not yet melted, remained on the ground; drifting against a nearby stone wall. It was exciting when a Franciscan Friar walked by; even more so, for some reason, when he unexpectedly brought his hood up!

### In the Footsteps of the Saint

We walked to the *Papal Basilica of St. Francis of Assisi*, the Mother Church of the original Franciscan *Order of Friars Minor*. Here St. Francis' body was hidden for fifty years after his death.

Such were the times, Franciscans feared attempts by other Orders to steal it for what were then considered valuable relics. We realized we were standing where Francis had stood, walking where he had walked, and seeing what he had seen.

### The Basilica of St. Francis of Assisi

Knowing this, and that the buildings and scenery were virtually unchanged from his time, was intense and exhilarating. Reaching the Church we paused to take it all in.

The building of this Basilica was begun in 1228 A.D., the year Francis was canonized as a saint; just two years after his death at age 44. The Upper Church was closed for repairs, due to the partial collapse of the roof during a recent earthquake.

We were able to look through the main doors and see inside.

### A Habit St. Francis Wore

Touring the Lower Church, we were entranced by Giotto's beautiful frescoes. Beneath the Lower Church, we visited the crypt where the "little *poverello*" (poor one) is laid to rest.

In awe we viewed, preserved under glass, the very Habit, or robe, that St. Francis was wearing when he went home to be with the Lord. Everything in Assisi deeply touched and affected us.

# 1.2  Ireland: Celtic Missionary Monks

*"The Sacred Three, my fortress be.*
*Encircling me, come and be*
*'round my hearth and my home."*

-Old Celtic Prayer

### Robert and Lupe

January of 1999 found us visiting Ireland, one of my wife Linda's ancestral homes. Along the country's far western coast, ruins of a castle or monastery are seen seemingly every five miles.

Linda's father, Robert, who we affectionately called Lay Monk Bob, was a McCarthy. Both of his parents were born in Ireland. Linda's mother, Lupe, was born in San Luis Potosi, and grew up in León, Guanajuato, both in Mexico.

The two met when Robert was a Trolley Car driver in San Francisco, and Linda's mother entered and sat down. It was love at first sight. At that time, Bob spoke no Spanish, and Lupe spoke no English.

### Monastery Ruins

In farmers' fields, cows grazed peacefully under the one or two stone walls still standing, where the Rose Window of a monastery church, now empty of its colored glass, was silhouetted against the lush pastoral landscape.

Traveling across the entire island, we completed our journey at high rocky cliffs overlooking the gray Atlantic. From here, as the Irish like to say:

*"The next parish over is Boston."*

We visited many monastery ruins, and saw several of the early Celtic monks' unique beehive-shaped stone huts.

These had been assembled without mortar, yet were entirely waterproof. This was achieved merely by the careful placement of correctly shaped stones.

## Gallerus Oratory and Skellig Michael

Here too, we prayed in the Gallerus Oratory, a small stone chapel barely large enough for twelve monks. It is the oldest un-restored Church in the world, and has stood on this spot for over 1,400 years.

Nearby Mt. Brandon is named for monk Brendan the Navigator. From the monastery he founded on its peak, Brendan planned the voyages that may have taken him as far as North America.

Only slightly over seven miles off of this coast, the monks of Skellig Michael lived and prayed for over six hundred years.

That great mysterious and mystical rock, rising 714 feet straight up out of the ocean, has long been known as the monastery "halfway to Heaven."

## Croagh Patrick

This far western coast is where St. Patrick was brought to, from his home in Roman Britain, after being kidnapped by Irish slave traders. Here Patrick served as a slave for six years, tending sheep, from the age of sixteen until the age of twenty-two.

In this part of Ireland, Patrick climbed the mountain now named after him: *Croagh Patrick*. Beginning from this very spot, over the next three decades he would convert the entire island of Ireland to Christianity.

Everywhere he went, Patrick founded monastic communities that would become great centers of teaching and learning.

# 1.3 Prayer & Christ's Great Commission

*"Cha robh dithis riamh a' fadadh teine nach do las eatarra."*

*"Two never kindled a fire, but it lit between them."*

-Old Gaelic Proverb

———

*"For where two or three are gathered in My name,
there am I in the midst of them."*

-Matthew 18:20

## Lives Saturated in Prayer

Linda and I have lived as Lay Monks in the ancient Celtic monastic lifestyle since 1999. What affect does it have on a person to dedicate themselves to a life of prayer, and then to live out that dedication for nearly two decades of their life?

The answer would no doubt be different for every Christian. For us, the practice and study of prayer led us naturally into the study of Francis of Assisi and the ancient Celtic monks. These many inspiring men and women of prayer included:

*Ninian of Caledonia, Patrick of Ireland, Brigid of Kildare, Ita of Killeedy, Brendan the Navigator, Kevin of Glendalough, Columba of Iona, Aidan of Lindisfarne, Hilda of Whitby, Cuthbert of Lindisfarne, Columbanus of Leinster, David of Wales, Samson of Wales, and The Venerable Bede.*

## A History of Prayer

All of these male and female monastics lived intensely holy lives, saturated in prayer, in Scripture, and in Scripture memorization. Many were *evangelistic missionary Christians* who brought the good news of the Gospel to others; in their own, and in many other countries. This research into historical teaching on prayer, brought us into the study of basic essential Christian doctrine. It led us into intense reading and study of the Bible, and much memorization of Scripture.

Learning about these ancient Celtic Christian men and women of prayer also took us into the study of the even earlier Christians that *they* had studied: the Early Church, the Desert Fathers, and the Church Fathers. All of their lives created in us a desire to emulate the practice of personal godliness and purity of every one of them.

### Prayer and Evangelism

The life histories of many great men and women of prayer were inspirational in our own commitment to evangelism and missionary work, in the fulfilling of Christ's Great Commission. We were greatly blessed by reading the stories of their lives. Many of these men and women of prayer were Missionaries, Evangelists, and Pastors, who also followed our Lord's command to:

*"...go into all the world*
*and proclaim the Good News to everyone."*

-Mark 16:15

### We Entered Deeply Into the Practice of Prayer

For nearly twenty years we have read as many books on prayer as we could; books written over the past two thousand years. Study of prayer drew us into a study of Protestant History, and of the various Denominations.

We discovered many great men and women of God. Our studies included the lives of Protestant Reformers, and the founders of historic Christian religious movements. What we learned was that these inspiring Christians had all made prayer central to their lives and ministries.

# 1.4 The Early Church & Dietrich Bonhoeffer

*"The awareness of a spiritual tradition
that reaches through the centuries
gives one a certain feeling of security
in the face of all transitory difficulties."*

*"Action springs not from thought,
but from a readiness for responsibility."*

*"We must be ready to allow ourselves
to be interrupted by God."*

-Dietrich Bonhoeffer (1906-1945)

———

*"The blood of martyrs is the seed of the Church."*

-Tertullian (c. 200 A.D.)

### Prayer and Godliness

In researching the early centuries immediately following the New Testament era, we learned of many more prayerful men and women of God. Was there another common denominator in all of their lives besides the love of God and of prayer?

Yes. Not outwardly, in their individual callings, but inwardly, in their living lives of true personal holiness.

In the earliest centuries of Christianity, many of those dedicated to God chose to become monastics.

We found ourselves more and more affected by the Scriptural godliness and purity that they practiced in their day to day lives.

As our Lord taught:

*"Blessed are the pure in heart, for they shall see God."*

-Matthew 5:8

35

## Martyrs

Purity of heart results in purity of thought, which leads to purity in word and deed. It is attainable solely by grace from the Father, through Christ, in the power of the Holy Spirit.

We entered ever more deeply into the practice of prayer. There was another common denominator in the lives of these ancient saints: all had given up their own lives in total dedication to Christ.

Many suffered much for the sake of the Gospel. Some even paid the ultimate price of martyrdom.

## The Beginning of Life

Dietrich Bonhoeffer was a Lutheran Pastor in Germany. He helped smuggle Jewish people out of Germany and into Switzerland. He openly criticized Hitler and the Nazi Party when speaking on the radio.

In 1943 he was implicated in a conspiracy to assassinate Adolf Hitler, and was arrested by the Gestapo. He was a prisoner for two years in the Buchenwald and Flossenburg Concentration Camps.

At Flossenburg, on April 9, 1945, immediately after he conducted his final worship service for the other prisoners, the Nazis executed Dietrich by hanging. His last words were:

*"This is the end – for me the beginning of life."*

## *"The Cost of Discipleship"*

The Allies liberating Germany reached the Flossenburg Camp only seven days later. Upon learning that the American soldiers would soon arrive, the Nazis executed all of the prisoners, a standard Nazi policy, that thankfully they did not always have time to carry out.

Germany would unconditionally surrender three weeks later.

S.G. Preston


In his classic book, *The Cost of Discipleship*, written in 1936, Lutheran Theologian Dietrich Bonhoeffer spoke favorably of the *Old* Monasticism (p.46):

> *"Monastic life thus became a living protest*
> *against the secularization of Christianity,*
> *against the cheapening of grace."*

## A New Monasticism

Earlier, on January 14, 1935, in a letter to his brother, Karl-Friedrick, Dietrich had written even more favorably of a *New* Monasticism:

> *"...the restoration of the church will surely come only from a new*
> *type of monasticism which has nothing in common with the old*
> *but a complete lack of compromise*
> *in a life lived in accordance with the*
> *Sermon on the Mount*
> *in the discipleship of Christ.*
>
> *I think it is time to gather people together*
> *to do this..."*

# 1.5  Boston Globe Articles: *"The unexpected monks..."*

*"It's the Holy Spirit's job to convict.*
*God's job to judge, and my job to love."*

-Billy Graham

———

*"In essentials unity.  In nonessentials liberty.*
*In all things love."*

-Rupertus Meldenius
German Reformed Lutheran
(Written in 1627)

## Born Again Protestant Monks

On Feb. 3, 2008, *The Boston Globe* published Molly Worthen's article: *The unexpected monks...* with her accompanying sidebar article: *In the beginning...*

The complete articles are on our website *PrayerFoundation Lay Monks™* (*www.prayerfoundation.net*), and on the *Boston Globe's* website.

We have posted all of the excellent photos by world-class photographer Leah Nash that accompanied the original article, but the *Boston Globe* did not.  She also took the photo used for the front cover of this book, at the same time in 2008.

Molly Worthen holds a PH.D. from Yale in American Religious History, and is currently Assistant Professor of History at the University of North Carolina, Chapel Hill.

## Evangelical Monasticism

Writing with the objectivity of the historian, Prof. Worthen has done a masterful job in these articles.  She points out that the reason the concept of Evangelical Monks is startling to many Evangelicals, is at least partly due to monasticism having been so totally rejected during the Protestant Reformation of the 16th century.

Interestingly enough, most Protestants are totally unaware that Martin Luther, himself a former Augustinian monk, had originally considered keeping the monasteries as schools, and only later rejected the idea.

## Why Luther Rejected Monasticism

Luther's rejection of monasticism, involved an association in his time with a doctrine of forgiveness of sins, and a comparison with baptism.

It was taught that becoming a monk removed all previous sins, *in the same way that it was believed baptism did.* The Protestant Reformers rightly rejected these comparisons to baptism.

## Knights of Prayer Lay Monks ™

Below are a few brief excerpts from the articles (quotations Copyright 2008 *Globe Newspaper Company*). The Words in parentheses have been added for clarity:

*"S.G. Preston is a Knight of Prayer.*

*Each morning at his Vancouver, Washington home, he wakes up and prays one of the 50-odd psalms he has committed to memory, sometimes donning a forest green monk's habit...monastic traditions loom large in* (his) *daily routine, yet* (he is) *an evangelical Protestant...*

*There is now a growing movement to revive evangelicalism by reclaiming parts of* (Early Church) *tradition - including monasticism.*

*Some 100 groups that describe themselves as both evangelical and monastic have sprung up in North America..."*

## Desiring More Than Televangelists

Molly Worthen accurately records the charge of much of New Monasticism that portions of evangelicalism have become shallow, superficial, and overly commercial:

*"In an era in which televangelists and megachurches
dominate the face of American evangelicalism,
offering a version of Christianity*

*inflected by populist aesthetics and the gospel of prosperity,
the rise of the New Monastics suggests that mainstream worship
is leaving some people cold...*

*The New Monastics come from a variety of religious backgrounds,
from Presbyterian to Pentecostal.*

*All share a common frustration with what they see as the over
commercialized and socially apathetic culture of mainstream
evangelicalism."*

## Rejection of Shallow Spirituality

New Monastic Scott Bessenecker, in his book, *The New Friars* comments on what he considers to be:

*"...spiritual flabbiness in the broader church
and a tendency to assimilate into a corrupt,
power-hungry world..."*

Prof. Worthen goes on to document that many mainstream Evangelicals are all too aware of the same problems that the New Monasticism movement sheds light on:

*"A recent study by Willow Creek Community Church in Illinois -
one of the most influential megachurches in the nation –*

*discovered that many churchgoers felt stalled in their faith,
alienated by slick, program-driven pastors*

40

*who focus more on niche marketing
than cultivating contemplation.*

*The study suggested that megachurch members know how to belt
out jazzy pop hymns from their stadium seats, but they don't always
know how to talk to God alone."*

## Back to the Basics

The solution offered is a dedication to prayer and simple Christian living. Monasticism is seen as a metaphor for such a life. We certainly agree with this view.

Perhaps it is best summed up by Jonathan Wilson-Hartgrove in his book:

*New Monasticism: What It Has to Say to Today's Church...*

*"The real radicals aren't quoting Che Guevara or listening to
Rage Against the Machine on their iPods. The true revolutionaries
are learning to pray."*

## Monks in the World

Prof. Worthen accurately documents the beliefs of many New Monastics, including our own. She writes:

*"...the Knights of Prayer, for example, are not interested in
liberalizing movements within the church... New Monastics
consider themselves 'monks in the world.'*

*They are not interested in extreme isolation or asceticism...nearly
all have regular jobs and social lives. From the traditionalist
perspective, many break the most essential monastic rule: they are
married.*

*Five centuries of Protestant heritage have alienated most New
Monastics from the notion of religiously motivated celibacy.*

*More importantly, these groups do not aim to separate themselves from society – on the contrary, they see New Monasticism as a means to better integrate core Christian values into their lives as average citizens."*

## Celtic Monks, Franciscan Friars, The New Celtic Franciscans

In her insightful accompanying sidebar article, *"In the beginning...,"* Molly Worthen's research has uncovered important information about the motivational sources behind much of New Monasticism. She writes:

*"New Monastics find inspiration in two very different strands of...religious life: the ancient...Celtic monks, and the wandering Franciscan friars.*

*New Monastics have picked up on the popular renaissance of Celtic culture underway in America for the past 20 years.*

*Vancouver, Washington based evangelicals S.G. Preston and his wife, Linda, were inspired to found their monastic order, The Knights of Prayer, after visits to Ireland, and Assisi, St. Francis' homeland...*

## Missionary Monks

*The Celtic monks 'were like Billy Graham,' Preston said. 'They were missionary monks - totally different from the Middle Ages kind of thing, when monks wanted to go on retreat against the world.'"*

*While the Prestons consider their monastic order a 'prayer encouragement ministry,' a Web-based mission that provides resources and structure for evangelical individuals interested in monastic spirituality* (with other New Monastics they also) *cite the more activist model of the Franciscans..."*

We recorded and saved the comments of the Franciscan Friars on the EWTN (*Eternal Word Television Network*) talk show, *Life On the Rock,* when they spoke about The Prayer Foundation *Knights of Prayer Monks*™ and the fact that we often refer to ourselves as Celtic Franciscans.

The Friars said:

*"Even Protestants love St. Francis!"*

## Preaching Friars

Of course, it's true. What's not to love? St. Francis loved animals. He once even preached a sermon to the birds! In the Catholic Church, St. Francis has been named the official Patron Saint of Animals, and of Ecology. He fed the poor and cared for the sick.

Seeing someone dressed more poorly than himself, Francis would exchange clothes with them. He fed, hugged, and kissed lepers, and manifested Christ's love to everyone he came in contact with.

Even atheists seem to love him. In fact, almost everyone does. Most Evangelical Protestants find themselves drawn to him.

As Mark Van Steenwyk, a Minneapolis New Monastic, correctly points out:

*"It's easier for evangelicals to connect with Franciscans because the Franciscan order is a preaching order.*
*The evangelical impulse is there."*

# 1.6 Memorizing & Praying the Psalms

*"We must imitate Christ's life and his ways if we are to be truly enlightened and set free from the darkness of our own hearts.*

*Let it be the most important thing we do."*

-Thomas à Kempis (1380-1471) Augustinian Monk
Member, *Brethren of the Common Life*
Author: *The Imitation of Christ*

### The Imitation of Christ

Thomas à Kempis' book, *The Imitation of Christ*, is the most printed book in the world after the Bible. This book was influential in slave ship Captain John Newton's conversion to Christianity (author of the lyrics to *Amazing Grace*).

*The Imitation of Christ* was Thomas' instruction book for the Novice Monks in his Augustinian monastery. John Wesley, the Founder of the Methodists, stated that he believed it to be the best summary of the Christian life that he had ever read.

Billy Graham said it was his favorite book, after the Bible. Dr. Graham even kept a copy of it on his nightstand. Now we are talking about *Evangelical Monasticism!*

### A Personal Prayer Tip:

### Imitating Christ by Memorizing and Praying Psalms

Memorization of Scripture is a large and very important part of our Christian life, especially of our prayer life. Memorization of psalms for use in prayer is a key biblical practice; observed by Old and New Testament believers for the past 3,000 years.

The book of *Psalms* is the Prayer Book of the Church. Historically, monastics have memorized all 150 Psalms, praying through all of them once each week.

## Psalm 23 and Psalm 117

If you only memorize one psalm, the 23rd Psalm would be almost everyone's first and favorite choice. Or, you might want to begin with Psalm 117; it is the shortest psalm: only two verses long!

We have memorized both The 23rd Psalm and Psalm 117, word for word directly from the *King James Version* of the Bible, and pray them daily. Of course, you could use any version of the Bible that you prefer.

## Athanasius and Luther

Bishop Athanasius of Alexandria (c. 296-373 A.D.) and Martin Luther (1483-1546) both taught that Christians should pray the Psalms.

We like the practice of praying five psalms a day, praying through all 150 every month. We do not require this of anyone, but we do recommend it. This was Billy Graham's own practice. It too, is Evangelical Monasticism! Dr. Graham said:

*"One half of all the quotes
that Jesus made from the Old Testament
came from the book of Psalms,
because the Psalmist lived every experience that we live."*

*"I used to read five psalms every day –
that taught me how to get along with God.
Then I read a chapter of Proverbs every day,
and that taught me how to get along
with my fellow man."*

## Praying One Different Psalm Every Day

If praying five psalms a day is not always possible, a good alternative practice is to resolve to pray at least one different psalm per day; to continue praying them in order until all 150 have been prayed; and then to begin over again. Even if *only one* different psalm is prayed every day, you would be praying through all 150 psalms, twice each year.

This is a spiritually beneficial lifetime practice for any Christian.

## What Do Great Lives of Prayer Share In Common?

All observed regular, daily times of prayer. They flooded Heaven with prayer and received answers to prayer on an almost daily basis.

*New Monasticism, Evangelical Monasticism, Celtic Lay Monasticism.* There is an ever-growing interest worldwide in historic monastic practice, and an ever-growing interest in prayer.

You are reading or listening to this book because you have that interest. You desire to draw near to God through prayer, and through His Word. This is also my prayer for you. May God bless you as you pursue your own *great life of prayer*.

\* \* \*

## C.S. Lewis (1898-1963) Writing On Prayer:

*'Relying on God has to begin all over again every day as if nothing had yet been done."*

*"It doesn't change God. It changes me."*

*"It is much easier to pray for a bore than to go visit him."*

*"Some people feel guilty about their anxieties and regard them as a defect of faith. I don't agree at all. They are afflictions, not sins."*

*"For prayer is request. The essence of request is that it may or may not be granted."*

*"For most of us the prayer in Gethsemane is the only model. Removing mountains can wait."*

*"Meantime, however, we want to know not how we should pray if we were perfect, but how we should pray being as we now are...It is no use to ask God with factitious earnestness for A when our whole mind is in reality filled with the desire for B. We must lay before Him what is in us: not what ought to be in us."*

*"I sometimes pray not for self-knowledge in general but for just so much self-knowledge at the moment as I can bear and use at the moment; the little daily dose."*

*"The most valuable thing the Psalms do for me is to express the same delight in God which made David dance."*

*"A concentrated mind and a sitting body make for better prayer than a kneeling body and a mind half asleep."*

\* \* \*

## *Answers to Prayer*
*PrayerFoundation™ 24-Hr. Prayerchain*

### Oct. 22, 2001 - Answer to Prayer:

My little grandson Nicco, 4 1/2 years old, was diagnosed with an inoperable brainstem tumor in November of '99, just two months before he turned 3. After 11 months of heavy chemo, he could not even walk.

At this point the doctors were worried the tumor was growing again, and put him on six weeks of radiation. A month later when he had his next MRI the doctors realized that the tumor had been shrinking all along.

They say they cannot explain this. But we know that all the prayers for Nicco have been heard, and that is why the tumor has shrunk.

Thank you and God bless you all.

*-Thordis*

---

(From the book: *Answers to Prayer* by S.G. Preston)

# 2: *Prayer, Essence of the Christian Life*

## 2.1  Prayer in the Night: Psalm 134

> *"The monks asked Abba Agathon,*
> *'Among all of our different practices,*
> *which requires the most effort?'*
>
> *Monk Agathon answered,*
> *'I think that there is nothing*
> *more difficult than praying to God.*
>
> *For each time a person begins to pray,*
> *their enemies, the demons, attempt to stop them;*
> *for the demons know that nothing hinders them*
> *as much as praying to God.*
>
> *In everything else a person attempts,*
> *if they don't stop, they eventually receive rest.*
> *But to pray, a person must strive*
> *until their very last breath."*

-Sayings of the Desert Fathers
Egyptian Desert (3rd Century A.D.)

**3 a.m.**

Nearly every night around 3 a.m., I wake up. Leaving the lights off, because everyone else is still asleep, I carefully go downstairs and let Hermiston, our Scottish Terrier, outside.

He has been trained, that when he goes outside, he knows not to make any noise if it is before 9 a.m. or after 9 p.m.

Between those times he can sometimes be, as the Dog Show announcers say, "quite vocal." Meaning: "barks a lot." He is a very lovable dog; the third Hermiston we have had.

49

We adopted the first near Hermiston, Oregon; so the name. In a few minutes, he'll be waiting quietly at the door to come in.

## Prayer in the Chapel

Our monastery in Vancouver, Washington is a large three-story house on three-quarters of an acre, situated in a very quiet and peaceful cul-de-sac. In our Chapel, the moonlight is shining in through twelve-foot high windows with stained glass vines and grape clusters at the very top.

The original monastery building we began our ministry in, was a much smaller house located just across the Columbia River in Portland, Oregon. Our move to Vancouver, Washington took place in September of 2004.

## Prayer in the Night

I remove my slippers before entering the Chapel. Though long past midnight, I pray Psalm 119:62...

> *"At midnight I will rise to give thanks to You,*
> *because of Your righteous judgments."*

And sing Psalm 134 silently to God:

> *"Behold, bless ye the LORD,*
> *all ye servants of the LORD;*
> *which by night, stand in the house of the LORD.*
> *Lift up your hands in the Sanctuary, and bless the LORD.*
> *The LORD, that made heaven and earth,*
> *bless thee out of Zion."*

I will pray for about half an hour, including spontaneous prayer, and return to bed.

S.G. Preston

## 2.2 Our Monastery Chapel

*"The breath of prayer comes from the life of faith."*

-John Mason (1646-1694)
Calvinist Anglican Priest

———

*"But who would hesitate every day
to prostrate themselves before God;
at least in the first prayer
with which we enter on the daylight?"*

-Tertullian (Written c. 200 A.D.)

**6 a.m.**

It is now 6 a.m. and the alarm is sounding. This time when I wake up, I may be slightly groggy. I let Hermiston out again, and head for the Chapel.

Our Chapel has a vaulted ceiling that comes to a traditional Church peak. It is not quite two stories tall; about 16 feet high.

There is a very nice second-story balcony overhanging the back wall. The floor of the room itself is 13 ft. by 14 ft., and an enormous red Persian carpet covers the entire floor in front of the altar.

Our Chapel, the largest room in the monastery, which originally began as our completely empty Prayer Room, has gradually, over the past fourteen years, acquired an interesting mix of styles.

We felt led to add first one thing, and then another.

The altar is in the historic western Christian rectangular style, similar to those found in Lutheran, Anglican, and Roman Catholic Churches.

The hanging oil lamps on the walls and the central chandelier are of glass and brass in the Byzantine style.

51

**Japanese Furnishings**

Traditional Japanese design can be seen in the large bell stand, which I designed and built myself, and in the tatami mats and seat pillows that encircle the walls, and the central carpet. The bell stand is 4 ft. 9 in. tall; the bell itself is 18 in. high.

Why Japanese? My sister lived in Japan for many years. My niece and nephew were born there. Lay Monk Linda and I have worked in Sapporo, Japan, when we were chosen as one of six Craft businesses to represent our Market there.

In Japan we were introduced to the Mayor of Sapporo and to the United States Ambassador to Japan. They both requested that I draw them, and I gave each of them their drawings as gifts.

**Visiting Kyoto**

When our work in Sapporo was completed, we decided to stay in Japan for a while longer, and visited both Kyoto and nearby Nara, two cities that have been preserved intact and untouched for a millennium.

The time of Kyoto's prominence was from 794-1185 A.D. This was the era of feudal Japan; the Edo Period of the Shoguns. Kyoto was the ancient Imperial capital of Japan for over 1,000 years.

It is considered by the Japanese people to be *"the heart of Japan."*

During WWII, the American Military ordered that these two cities not be bombed, because of their value as historic sites.

**Praying in the Garden**

I also used to live near the *Portland Japanese Garden*, and as a member, was allowed entry before it opened to the public at 9 a.m. every morning. An hour a day, for over a decade, I prayed the Psalms there from memory. I would be one of eight people in the garden, four of which would be gardeners.

52

Each day, I would choose a different place to sit: viewing a splashing stream, a quiet pond, or a rushing waterfall.

## Prayer and Rain

It rains in the Pacific Northwest from mid-September until mid-June. Temperatures average 40-60 degrees, even in January and February, due to the warm North Pacific Current (the North Pacific Drift).

Rain in the Pacific Northwest is usually a mist, and does not have much effect on how people here live their lives. Locals almost never carry umbrellas. If you see somebody with one, they are likely a visiting tourist.

If it is raining, as it does five days out of seven all winter, I would sit beneath one of the many covered areas placed throughout the garden for that purpose.

The Portland Japanese Garden is a very beautiful and peaceful place to pray.

# 2.3 Chapel Candles, Incense, Oil Lamps

*"Worshippers never leave church…*
*we carry our sanctuary with us wherever we go."*

-A.W. Tozer (1897-1963)
Pastor, Evangelist, Theologian, Author
Christian & Missionary Alliance

## Byzantine Oil Lamps

The two large candlesticks on the Altar (or Communion Table, or Holy Table) are replicas of ones in the Cathedral of Notre Dame on the Isle de Cité in Paris.

Two candlesticks have historically symbolized the two natures of Christ, representing His complete divinity and His complete humanity.

We were blessed to be able to visit the Cathedral when we were in France.

I have mentioned the oil lamps found throughout the Chapel. Seven Greek Orthodox lamps are mounted on the walls, and a Russian Orthodox Chandelier hangs from the ceiling in the center of the room.

All have floating wicks, and we burn only olive oil in them.

## A Pure Offering

A large golden censer is swung during worship services from its three long chains (symbolizing the Trinity).

When not sending out clouds of sweet-smelling incense, it rests centered between the two large candlesticks in front of the Celtic Cross.

Its use by us is a small part of the fulfillment of this prophecy from Holy Scripture:

> *" 'For from the rising of the sun, to its setting,*
> *My name shall be great among the Gentiles;*
> *and in every place incense*
> *shall be offered to My name,*
> *and a pure offering:*
> *for My name shall be great among the nations,'*
> *says the LORD of Hosts."*

-Malachi 1:11

The *"pure offering"* refers to the observance of Communion, which fulfills the commandment of our Lord:

> *"Do this in remembrance of Me."*

-Luke 22:19

**All Glory to God**

The *Worship Service* I compiled for our Order's own use, is based on worship services going back to the third century. There is not much *detailed* information before then about what was actually said during worship, only brief outlines of the service as a whole.

In our Service we use a smaller set of three golden bells connected to one handle, which we ring three times during the part of the liturgy where the words, *"Holy, Holy, Holy"* (Isaiah 6:3; Revelation 4:8) are addressed to God:

> *"Holy, Holy, Holy; Lord God Almighty:*
> *heaven and earth are filled with Your glory!*
>
> *Blessed is He who arrives*
> *in the Name of the LORD!*
> *Hosanna in the Highest!*
>
> *Blessed is He who arrives*
> *in the Name of the LORD!"*

## Incense

On each side of the altar are two small hand-crafted pottery jars containing incense.

One jar contains pure frankincense, a tree resin found only in the Near East, and the other holds a different fragrance of incense.

We change them every few months, as each kind is used. Our incense is obtained from Orthodox monks.

(Note: We are an Interdenominational Ministry; we ourselves like to attend local Church Services as often as we can, but the wonderful Church we attend is not Liturgical, and having our own Liturgical Service sometime during the week fulfills that desire.)

## The Holy Scriptures

On the left side of the Chapel is a pulpit (*ambo*), with a large family size *King James Bible* open on it.

We also read from a *New King James Version* Bible, and an English Standard Version Bible.

In our personal worship, our favorite Version to memorize from is the *King James Version*.

To read from on our own, we prefer the *English Standard Version* (ESV).

The exception is, although I had already memorized Psalms 1-25 from the *King James Version*, after I completed an *updated King James Version* of these psalms, I also memorized the new versions.

This was not as difficult as it sounds, because my goal was to change as little as possible, only what was absolutely necessary for increased clarity and understanding.

Also, I love memorizing, especially the *Psalms*.

And praying the *Psalms*, or other Scripture, is my favorite way to pray.

S.G. Preston

**A House of Prayer**

To the right of the altar is a gothic wood stand holding a large pottery bowl containing sand. It is there to hold candles lit and placed by individuals.

The altar, pulpit, and stand for the bowl filled with sand are all covered with cloth the color of the current Church Season and embroidered with Christian symbols. The liturgical term for these colored cloths is: *paraments*.

White is the color used during the Easter and Christmas Seasons. Both Seasons are preceded, respectively, by the two 6-week fasting Seasons of Lent and Advent. Yes, we observe them! The color for both Lent and Advent is purple, the historic color of repentance.

**Advent and Celtic Advent**

Advent is a Church Season, first observed by the ancient Celtic Christians of Gaul. It was later adopted by the entire Christian Church. It celebrates the two *Advents*, or *Arrivals*, of Christ.

The ancients emphasized his Return at the end of the age, while Christians today emphasize his first Advent, in Bethlehem, the baby born for our Salvation.

The season lasts six weeks, from Nov. 15th until Christmas. It actually begins at sundown on November 14th and lasts until Midnight Christmas Eve/Christmas Day.

These are the dates observed by Celtic Christians and Eastern Orthodox when celebrating it; the dates that the Roman Catholic Church also originally followed.

We celebrate ancient *Celtic Advent*, which has the same dates as Orthodox Advent. Orthodox also call it *Nativity Fast*, or *St. Philip's Fast*. Eastern Orthodoxy has its own specific observances regarding fasting during this season. We do not require any of the Lay Monks of our Order, or anyone else, to observe either Advent or Celtic Advent.

## Western Advent

In the 10th century, Pope Gregory I (the Great), shortened Advent by two weeks, and made the beginning date change from year to year. We refer to this as *Western Advent*.

The historic Reformation Protestant Churches retained this observance, keeping the shortened Roman Catholic dates, but omitting the fasting. The Catholic Church, 450 years later also omitted the fasting, at Vatican II, held from 1962-1965.

## Advent Wreaths, Candles, and Calendars

Many Protestants celebrate Advent, using an Advent Wreath with Advent Candles, and an Advent Calendar. The Calendar is especially fun for children, as one little "door" of the Calendar is opened each day, and inexpensive Advent Calendars can be obtained with a small toy or piece of chocolate behind each door.

(Note: In *Liturgical Time*, each new day begins and ends at sundown. This was the Jewish custom of reckoning time, and was continued by the Christian Church.)

## Church Season Colors

These are the colors generally used in Western (Protestant and Catholic) Churches.

The rest of the Church Year is known as Ordinary Time, though this term is not used in all Churches, and its color is green.

There are a few exceptions: Lutherans use blue instead of purple for Advent, and some churches additionally use red during Holy Week, the week immediately before Easter.

Eastern Orthodox Churches use darker or lighter colors for the different Church Seasons, rather than specific colors, and therefore the specific colors used will be different than those in Western Churches.

Upon entering our Chapel, I make the Sign of the Cross, invoking the Trinity:

*"In the Name of the Father, and of the Son,
and of the Holy Spirit. Amen."*

-Matthew 28:19

## Chapel Lights

Going to the altar, I top off the olive oil in the red glass Sanctuary Lamp hanging above it, a constantly lit symbol for the presence of the Holy Spirit.

Next, I choose a long, thin beeswax taper from beside the sand-filled pottery bowl. I light the candle and place it in the sand, again making the Sign of the Cross.

These candles have been made of 100% beeswax by Orthodox Nuns, who raise their own bees. When lit, the candles symbolize Christ as *the Light of the World* (John 8:12).

## Worship Service

In certain parts of our worship service we praise and pray in *responses* (omitting the references). Here is a small portion, compiled exclusively from Scripture, of Liturgy for our own use, original with me:

**Officiant:** *"Then Jesus lifted up His eyes toward heaven and prayed, 'Sanctify them through Your truth:*

**All:** *Your Word is truth.'"* (John 17:17)

**Officiant:** *"The entrance of Your Word gives light."* (Psalm 119:30)

**All:** *"Your Word is a light unto my path."* (Psalm 119:105)

**Officiant:** *"The spirit of a person is the candle of the LORD."* (Proverbs 20:27)

**All:** *"You will light my candle; the LORD my God will enlighten my darkness."* (Psalm 18:28)

## Hearing Billy Graham Speak In Person

Like nearly all Evangelicals, I consider Billy Graham to be the greatest Christian in my lifetime to be used by God for the fulfilling of Christ's Great Commission, and C.S. Lewis to be the greatest Christian writer.

In 1971, I attended the 100th Anniversary of the Moody Church in Chicago. Everyone was amazed when an unannounced guest speaker arrived: Billy Graham!

He was unannounced, because perhaps 10,000 Christians might have shown up to hear him speak, and the church could not hold that many people!

As it was, I was greatly blessed to see and hear Dr. Graham speak in such a relatively small (for Him) church venue.

Some might say that the Moody Church is not small at all, but instead is rather large. But it is quite small compared to the giant outdoor stadiums Billy Graham usually spoke at.

## A New Monasticism Chapel

When we began our ministry in 1999, we had not heard the term: "New Monasticism."

Yet in 2008, the *Boston Globe* newspaper included us in an article acknowledging us as one of its earliest ministries.

I have officiated at weddings held in our Chapel, and various Christian groups have visited to worship with us; sometimes bringing a guitar, or giving a teaching message; sometimes asking me to teach a class on prayer.

There are usually no pews or chairs in the Chapel, except when Lay Monk Bob was present, and then we brought one in for him.

**Traditional Hymns**

When we sang the old, traditional Hymns during our service, Bob would always accompany our singing by playing his harmonica.

He had several, and he was very good at playing them!

Lay Monk Bob, along with Lay Monk Danny (like David, "God's Musician"), was one of the four original members of our ministry. Lay Monk Bob (1926-2015) was with us until three years ago.

He had given his life to Christ at the age of nineteen, and after seventy years of service to God in evangelism, at nearly 89 years old, he went home to be with his Lord.

*"Cha bhi fios aire math an tobair*
*gus an traigh e."*

*"The value of the well is not known*
*until it goes dry."*

-Old Gaelic Saying

**Our Chapel Bell**

It was a great honor to know Lay Monk Bob, to pray and worship with him; to hear his comments concerning the Christian films we watched before our *Worship Service*.

The large memorial bell in our Chapel is dedicated to him, and we refer to it as *"Bob's Bell,"* or *"Monk Bob's Bell."*

There is a wonderful story behind this bell, because we consider it to be a *miracle* bell.

A Roman Catholic blacksmith named Mike made this beautiful bell as his gift to God, and in honor of St. Francis, to go in our small Franciscan Chapel (it is also a St. Patrick Chapel).

Mike was suffering from Cancer for several years, and could no longer do his blacksmith work, but he got up from his sickbed every day to work on this bell. We were unaware that he was doing this.

## When the Bell Rings

One day he simply showed up with this bell that he had made for God, and gave it to us, to place in the Chapel. It was two days before Memorial Day, when we were planning on visiting Lay Monk Bob's gravesite.

The bell is a beautiful brown color, which always makes us think of St. Francis, because of the Habit (robe) that Francis wore.

Whenever it rings, we will always think of Lay Monk Bob. Whenever it rings, we will always think of blacksmith Mike.

## Mother House

In the Mother House of our Order, the wonderful, beautiful Bell that Mike made, now rings several times daily.

# 2.4  6am: Awaking Prayer

*"Music's only purpose should be the glory of God
and the recreation of the human spirit."*

-Johann Sebastian Bach (1685-1750) Lutheran

## Prayer at Sunrise

In the Early Church, believers awoke at sunrise to pray.  They were able to do this because they lived relatively near the Equator; in the Near East, and around the Mediterranean.

The only time I ever did this consistently was when I was in Hawaii.

Most of the places in the nine states in which I have lived, have been much farther north, where sunrise varies considerably with the seasons.  Making a full prostration in our monastery Chapel, I lay flat on my face before God.

Rising to a kneeling position, I pray as a morning prayer, nine sections of verses from the Bible, that I have found to be most personally helpful in my Christian life.

Often, I will sing silently the songs written for the first two verses.

## Faithfulness

God is faithful, even when we are not.  We are not always faithful to God, but God is always faithful *to His Word* (2 Timothy 2:13).

His compassion is always available to us.  It is one of His "precious promises" (2 Peter 1:4).

I pray these verses from memory, in three groups of three verses (very Celtic!).  I pray just the verses, , not the references, although I have also memorized these.

I call these nine verses:

### *The Nine Affirmations*

**The First Three Affirmations Have to Do With *Forgiveness:***

*"This is the day that the LORD has made.
We will rejoice and be glad in it!"*

-Psalm 118:24

———

*"It is because of the LORD's mercies
that we are not consumed,
because His compassions fail not.*

*They are new every morning.
Great is Thy faithfulness!"*

-Lamentations 3:22-23

———

*"There is therefore now no condemnation
for those that are in Christ Jesus."*

-Romans 8:1

**The Second Three Affirmations Have to Do With *Prayer*:**

*"Evening, and morning, and at noon:
I will pray, and call out loud,
and He shall hear my voice."*

-Psalm 55:17

———

*"Cast all your cares upon Him,
for He cares for you."*

-1 Peter 5:7

S.G. Preston

----

*"Rejoice always, pray without ceasing,*
*in everything give thanks:*
*for this is the will of God in Christ Jesus concerning you."*

-1 Thessalonians 5:16-18

## The Third Three Affirmations Have to Do with Living the *Christian Life*:

*"All things work together for good, for those that love God."*

-Romans 8:28

----

*"I can do all things through Christ,*
*who strengthens me."*

*"Lord, what would you have me do today?"*

-Philippians 4:13; Acts 9:6

----

*"The fruit of the Spirit*
*is love, joy, peace;*
*patience, kindness, goodness;*
*faithfulness, humility, self-control."*

*"Since we live in the Spirit, let us also walk in the Spirit."*

-Galatians 5:22-23, 25

## Imitating the Angels

In the Early Church, books of the Bible were copied by hand on scrolls, making them extremely expensive. Unless you were fairly wealthy, and could afford one or more, you went to Church to hear the Bible read, and memorized what you desired to remember.

Several of the various psalms are designated as Morning Psalms in the biblical text. Many of these were used by Christians for morning prayer at one time or another in different eras.

Basil the Great (c. 330-379 A.D.) wrote:

> *"What is more blessed than to imitate on earth*
> *the choir of angels;*
> *at break of day to rise in prayer,*
> *and praise the Creator with anthems and songs;*
>
> *then go to labor in the clear radiance of the sun,*
> *accompanied everywhere by prayer,*
> *and seasoning work with praise, as if with salt?"*

# 2.5 Athanasius of Alexandria

*"The holy and inspired Scriptures*
*are sufficient of themselves*
*for the preaching of the truth."*

-St. Athanasius of Alexandria (c. 296-373 A.D.)
*"The Father of Orthodoxy"*
Attendant at the Adoption of the Nicene Creed
(325 A.D.)

**Morning Prayer**

With the grace that we have from Christ, you and I are free to pray whatever we prefer when we first awake. Some Christians like to pray the same prayer or prayers every day.

Others like to pray something different every day for a week, and then repeat the same sequence each week. Others still, like to alternate what they pray on different weeks.

Remember, that if you pray a different psalm every morning, you only repeat each one every five and a half months.

**Praying Psalm 5**

Many years ago, I read that Athanasius prayed Psalm 5 every morning, so I decided to try doing the same. Psalm 5 became my exclusive prayer every morning for five years. I still pray it most days, but no longer exclusively, and not every day. Now I begin to pray it once more, from memory:

*"Give ear to my words, O LORD;*
*consider my meditation.*
*Hear the sound of my cry, my King and my God; for to You I will*
*pray.*

*My voice You shall hear in the morning, O LORD.*
*In the morning I will direct my prayer to You,*
*and will look up."*

-Psalm 5:1-3

The last few verses are:

*"But let all those that put their trust in You rejoice.*
*Let them forever shout with joy,*
*because You defend them.*

*Let those also that love Your name,*
*be joyful in You.*
*For You, LORD, will bless the righteous.*
*With favor You will surround them, like a shield."*

-Psalm 5:11-12

## 325 A.D. - The Nicene Creed

Athanasius was present at the First Council of Nicaea (in today's Turkey), when the Nicene Creed was first formulated in 325 A.D.

He was Bishop of Alexandria for 45 years, from 328-373 A.D. For 17 of those years, he was exiled, while an Emperor who followed the Arian heresy sat on the throne: denying the Deity of Christ and the Trinity.

Bishop Athanasius was reinstated when Christian orthodoxy eventually triumphed. The Athanasian Creed is partly based on Athanasius' teachings, and was named for him. He was not its author.

## Ancient Bestsellers

Two books Athanasius wrote are classics, and have remained extremely popular even up through our own time.

S.G. Preston

The two are:

*On the Incarnation* and *The Life of Anthony*

The latter book records the life of Anthony the Great, *"The Father of Christian Monasticism."* Before writing his book, Athanasius traveled into the Egyptian desert just to meet Anthony, and was very impressed with his spirituality.

The book was a "best seller" of its time, and sparked the spread of a vibrant new movement in the Christian East, across North Africa, and throughout Europe: Christian Monasticism.

## No Monks in Europe

Before Athanasius' book, there were no monks in Europe. None. After…well, you already know…a Medieval Europe, Near East, and North Africa filled with Christian monks, monasteries, and monastic Orders.

St. Augustine would read Athanasius' book on Anthony, and decide to become a Christian.

## Walden Pond

From 1845-1847, Henry David Thoreau recorded his two years of living in a cabin in the woods. He built his cabin on Walden Pond, not far from Concord, Massachusetts. Thoreau wrote about these experiences in his book, *Walden, or My Life in the Woods.* One of his often quoted statements is:

*"How many a man has dated a new era in his life
from the reading of a book?"*

This was certainly true of myself. When I was sixteen years old, I read *Walden*.

One of Thoreau's goals was to live close to nature, and spend his time enjoying it. Another was to simplify his life down to the most important bare essentials.

## A Cheyenne Tipi

Desiring to have a similar experience, at the age of thirty, I bought a replica of a traditional Cheyenne Tipi. I was in Albuquerque, New Mexico at the time, and ordered it delivered General Delivery to Bozeman, Montana.

That was my final destination. Along the way, living in my camper truck, I visited nearly every National Park in the Rocky Mountains between New Mexico and Montana.

Arriving in Bozeman, I picked up the boxed canvas portions of my tipi at the Post Office. Next, I obtained a forestry permit to "cut firewood," cost: $5.00! Then I drove up dirt logging roads to the top of a mountain and harvested the 19 ft. lodgepole pines needed to set up my tipi. I didn't cut them up for firewood!

I lived in it for a year and two weeks, through all four seasons, like Thoreau did in his cabin at Walden (he actually lived in the cabin for two years, but when he wrote about his life there, he combined them into one year).

I pitched my tipi on top of a forested mountain in Montana, across the valley from a ski resort, and when winter ended, moved it to the Madison River, north of Yellowstone Park.

The Madison is one of the six best blue-ribbon trout fishing rivers in the entire world, and it was only ten feet from my front door-flap!

## Praying for Snow

People always asked me if it wasn't too cold in the winter? I had a fire, but the fire went out about 3:30 a.m. every night. The temperature was 20 below zero for a total of 28 days.

I would pray for snow. This was Montana, so snow would pile up two feet deep around the tipi, and stick to the canvas wall six inches deep. It was excellent insulation, for which I was very grateful. I was always happy when it snowed!

A tipi has an open smoke-hole at the top, about twelve feet up, so you can have a firepit and log fire in it. The downside was that some mornings I would wake up with a small pile of snow next to my head.

### Frostbitten Fingers

When the temperature hit a winter low of 35 below zero, I decided, yes, that it was now too cold. The wind-chill that day was 85 below, and walking five miles home to the tipi, three of my fingers became permanently frostbitten. My hands were in fur-lined gloves, deep in the pockets of an Air Force Parka, but the wind cut straight through it all. I had started living in the tipi just as Fall was beginning. When first Spring, and then Summer arrived, I found both seasons to be very pleasant, indeed.

### Tipi Animals

The ancient Celtic Monks have many stories having to do with wild animals. I think that if you live out in a wilderness area, and are not a hunter; and in addition, as a monastic, tend to be very quiet and very still; it is almost inevitable that many of the animals nearby will lose their fear of you.

My tipi was set up on a mountain slope, and the ground being very uneven, one of the lodgepoles was not as tight against the canvas as it should have been.

A squirrel regularly entered and left the tipi through the tipi's front door, using this lodgepole as a highway to and from his favorite tree.

In the morning when I went outside, I have seen a deer, barely twenty feet away, standing like a statue, watching me. Once I must have been very still indeed, because a rabbit entered the tipi and sat down next to me to rest.

## A Bull Elk

Another time, and again I must have been not making any movement at all.

I was sitting on the ground, reading a book outside, and looked up into the eyes of a bull Elk, towering over me with his head (and razor sharp antlers!) lowered to within three feet of me, staring into my face; staring into my eyes.

St. Francis and the ancient Celtic saints would no doubt have savored the moment: I was totally startled.

I think the Elk was just as startled when my head finally moved, which he had not been expecting.

But not startled enough to run away.

A full grown bull elk looks very large when you are seated cross-legged on the ground directly in front of one.

They are 5 feet tall *at the shoulder*, and weigh about 700 pounds!

As I slowly rose to my feet, the Elk didn't move, or take his eyes off me.

I backed away very slowly, the Elk advancing at exactly the same speed, maintaining exactly the same distance between us.

It took me at least twenty minutes to extricate myself from this predicament, by gradually increasing the distance between us, until I could get behind a tree.

I also had experiences with Black Bear, Coyotes, Rocky Mountain Goats, Bighorn Sheep, Moose, Buffalo, Grizzly Bears, and Bald Eagles.

But this is a book about prayer.

As an Old Gaelic Saying puts it:

*"Is sgeul eile sin."*
*"That's another story."*

72

S.G. Preston

**Reading the New Testament**

When I was nineteen, I had another experience where I:

> *"...dated a new era in my life*
> *from the reading of a book."*

And not just a new era, but a totally new life!

I read the New Testament through four times in a row, and then received Christ as my Lord and Savior.

# 2.6  From Monk Anthony to Monk Luther

*"For every man,*
*on every occasion,*
*can find in the Psalms*
*that which fits his needs,*
*which he feels to be appropriate;*
*as if they had been set there*
*just for his sake..."*

-Martin Luther (1483-1546)

**Preserving God's Word for Future Generations**

Over one-thousand years after Anthony lived, in Martin Luther's time, monasticism had become an older movement, in many places suffering from corruption and decay, superstition and un-Biblical practices.

That's how Luther saw it, with his background as an Augustinian monk. Technically, he was a *Friar*, like St. Francis, a member of a preaching or teaching Order.

Luther continued to wear his monastic habit for three years after his excommunication, until 1524. He had said that he would keep wearing it:

*"Until the world changed."*

Think of it! It took *only one* committed Christian, *only three years*, to change the world!

**Reformation Day**

On October 31, 1517, which many Protestants today celebrate as Reformation Day, Luther tacked up his list of *95 Theses* on the door of the Cathedral in Wittenburg, Germany.

The *95 Theses* listed what he saw as ninety-five errors in the Doctrine and Practice of the religious and Church life of his era.

Luther invited anyone to debate him on these problem areas, unaware that soon all of Europe would be joining the debate. Completely unaware that he had just begun the Protestant Reformation!

## Monk Luther

Most of us are familiar with what took place in history *after* Luther.

We may not be quite as familiar with what had happened *before* him, during the 1,200 years between Monk Anthony and Monk Luther.

Regrettably, for many Protestant Christians, this entire period of Christian history, from the end of the New Testament until the time of Luther, is one big blank; almost totally unknown.

Let's take a look...

In the fourth century, influenced by Anthony of Egypt, and using Pachomius' Rule as a guide, Basil the Great wrote a new Rule of monastic life.

He wrote it for the new monks of Cappadocia, in the Roman Province of Asia Minor (today's Turkey).

I quoted Basil earlier about imitating the choir of angels in Heaven by praising God in prayer every morning at sunrise.

## Monks On a Mission

Not long after this, monasteries were also founded in Gaul (now France).

From here, Ninian and Patrick would go out as missionary monks to convert, respectively, half of Scotland and all of Ireland to Christianity.

Beginning in the seventh century, and for the next several hundred years, the Irish monks who proliferated because of St. Patrick, would continuously send out thousands of missionary monks to the British Isles and to Continental Europe.

They would convert northern Europe to Christianity for the first time, and re-convert the southern half of Western Europe.

## Barbarians

But why did this part of Europe need to be re-converted to Christianity?

The western Roman Empire had long since collapsed, overrun by numerous barbarian hordes; including the Goths, Visigoths, Huns, and Vandals, who were now the new rulers, as well as a large proportion of the population.

These hordes had conquered Italy, barbarians ruling even the city of Rome from 476 A.D. on.

## Preserving Knowledge

One of the greatest achievements of the Irish Celtic Christian monks was to preserve the lost arts of reading and writing.

This knowledge had been lost throughout most of western Europe.

Irish monks would hand-copy the sacred texts of the Bible, and along with the Scribes in the Eastern Roman Empire of Byzantium, preserve God's Holy Scriptures for future generations.

S.G. Preston

# 2.7 Augustine of Hippo

*"Another kind of 'prayer without ceasing'*
*is longing.*

*Do not cease from prayer,*
*no matter what else you do,*
*if you are seeking after your day*
*of never-ending rest.*

*Do not allow your longing to end,*
*if you desire to never stop praying.*
*Longing is your unrelenting voice.*

*Your heart will become silent,*
*when love fades.*
*The call of your heart*
*is your blazing passion!*

*If longing consumes you forevermore,*
*you will keep calling out to God.*
*Then it will be certain*
*that God hears your cry,*
*when your love continues unabated."*

-St. Augustine, Bishop of Hippo (354-430 A.D.)
Author: *"Confessions"* and *"The City of God"*

## Monk, Bishop, Christian Writer

One of the first to embrace this ancient "New Monasticism" movement of the fourth century was a young man named Augustine.

He was from the Roman Empire's North African city of Hippo Regius. As I have already mentioned, Augustine had been reading Athanasius' new book, *The Life of Anthony*, just before he became a Christian.

Augustine decided that he too, wanted to become a monk. He would remain one for his entire life.

Later in life, Augustine would be acclaimed Bishop by the Christians in the Roman city of Hippo, in North Africa.

It may surprise many to learn that in the Early Church, for at least the first 400 years, Bishops were chosen not by the Church hierarchy, but by their own congregations.

## The City of God

In his lifetime, Augustine would write at least fifty books (perhaps 70!), including his autobiographical *Confessions*; and another classic work: *The City of God*.

The complete title is: *The City of God Against the Pagans*.

In this book, history is shown as conflict between the Earthly City, also called the City of Man, which will pass away at the end of time, and the City of God, which will triumph for all eternity under a victorious Christ.

His many works of Christian Theology would have a tremendous influence, not only on later Roman Catholic Churchmen, but also on Protestant Reformers like Martin Luther and John Calvin.

Along with Roman Catholicism, Eastern Orthodoxy acknowledges Augustine as one of the Church Fathers, even though the Orthodox do not agree with every aspect of his Theology.

## Evagrius of Pontus' Prayer Truth:

## Prayer and Theology Go Together

This saying of the monk Evagrius of Pontus (345-399 A.D.), is often quoted in the Orthodox Church:

> *"If you are a theologian you will pray truly.*
> *And if you pray truly, you are a theologian."*

The meaning being: that it is a waste of time to study *about* God, if you don't actually *know* God and *spend time with God in prayer.*

## Prayer and Love

Augustine himself had this to say about prayer:

*"True, whole prayer, is nothing but love."*

## A Martin Luther Prayer Tip:

## Let God Worry

Martin Luther, with half of Europe seeking his death, both the secular political powers and the Church Authorities, was only too aware of the absolute necessity and immense power of prayer. When Luther remarked that people: *"didn't acknowledge the great miracles God worked on Luther's behalf."*

I believe one of the things he was referring to was the fact that he was still alive. God is a miracle-working God. A great proof of this is that Luther died of old age.

He was not assassinated, and he was not burned at the stake. Luther had a saying, which was essentially a paraphrase of 1 Peter 5:7 (*"Cast all your cares upon Him, for he cares for you."*)

Luther's advice seems simplicity itself, and yet carries within it a vast wealth of Biblical spiritual depth and insight. Luther taught:

*"Pray, and let God worry."*

## John Calvin's Prayer Truth:

## Prayer Is Evidence of Inward Spirituality

The great men and women of God throughout history lived lives saturated in prayer.

If we do not grasp this, we will never really understand them, or understand what our own Christian life can and should be; for the Christian life is meant to be a life of prayer.

John Calvin (1509-1564), the French Reformer who lived on the shores of Lake Geneva, within view of the breathtakingly beautiful snow-covered Swiss Alps, saw a life of prayer as evidence of a true inward spirituality.

Calvin stated it this way:

*"The principle exercise*
*which the children of God have*
*is to pray.*

*For in this way they*
*give true proof of their faith."*

## 2.8 A Call to Holiness

*"Mol an látha math mu oidhche sibh."*

*"Praise the good day at night."*

-Old Gaelic Saying

**A Personal Prayer Tip:**

**Before Sleep Review the Day**

It is good every evening to praise God, thanking Him for all He has done:

> *"It is a good thing to give thanks to the LORD.*
> *To sing praises to Your Name, Most High:*
> *to declare Your lovingkindness every morning,*
> *and Your faithfulness every night."*

-Psalm 92:1-2

It is good every evening to go over what we have done wrong during the past day, trying to see how we might handle things differently; how we could have resisted particular temptations. This is a common practice among monks in Orthodox monasteries.

Sometimes we will see that if we had not put ourselves in *that position there*, the following temptation and fall to sin might have been resisted and avoided. Today this is often referred to as avoiding *"triggers."*

Reflecting on our day may let us become aware of areas in which we need to be more watchful, and where we need to pray for more grace: more help from God.

God desires to bring us closer to Himself in holiness and godliness; into a deeper relationship with Him.

## Prayer and the Trinity

Real Christian prayer is being in communion with God the Father, through the intercession of Christ, by the power of the Holy Spirit. It is a truly spiritual practice grounded in faith.

By definition, it is absolutely *not* something that we can do on our own, apart from God. This is truly *grace* (unmerited favor: unearned, undeserved). I have often heard Christian preachers and teachers ask this question:

> *"If the Holy Spirit were to be removed*
> *from our Christian service,*
> *would it make any difference*
> *in how we live our lives?"*

## Living the Christian Life

Are we working *for* God, in our own power, or *with* God as he leads us, moment by moment, in the power and under the guidance of the Holy Spirit?

Prayer, by its very nature, teaches us how our entire Christian life should be lived…in constant communion with our Creator. Hudson Taylor once explained:

> *"I used to ask God to help me.*
>
> *Then I asked if I might help Him.*
>
> *I ended up by asking Him*
> *to do His work through me."*

82

S.G. Preston

# 2.9  Partakers of the Divine Nature

*"But as He who has called you is holy,*
*you should also be holy in everything you do.*

*For it is written: 'Be holy, for I am holy."*

1 Peter 1:15-16

## All Things

G od's Word states that He has given us *"...all things that pertain to life and godliness."* And that by His promises we should be *"...partakers of the divine nature..."*
This verse is itself one of God's most amazing promises.

## Precious Promises

Athanasius of Alexandria, in his Easter letter written in 367 A.D., listed exactly the same 27 books as are currently found in the New Testament.

Yet early in the history of the Church, before the Canon of Scripture was closed, some Christians had argued that 2 Peter should not be a part of the Canon. I have no idea how anyone could read 2 Peter 1:3-4, and not realize it is Holy Scripture, the inspired Word of God:

*"According as His divine power has given to us*
*all things that pertain to life and godliness,*
*through the knowledge of Him who has called us*
*to glory and virtue;*

*by which are given to us*
*exceedingly great and precious promises;*

*that by these you might be partakers of the divine nature,*
*having escaped the corruption that is in the world*
*through evil desires."*

## Cleansed by God

Every week in our *Worship Service*, in the Liturgy of the Eucharist (Communion: *Eucharist* means *thanksgiving*), we recite together, from memory, these verses:

*"If we say that we have no sin,*
*we deceive ourselves,*
*and the truth is not in us.*
*If we confess our sins, He is faithful and just to forgive us our sins,*
*and to cleanse us from all unrighteousness."*

-1 John 1:8-9

## No Condemnation

Think of the wonderfully *clean* feeling you have when you step out of the shower. Often, though we know we are forgiven, we still feel terrible and defiled from the sin we have committed. When we receive God's forgiveness, we must also accept God's *cleansing*. The condemnation that we sometimes still feel is never from God:

*"For if our heart condemns us,*
*God is greater than our heart,*
*and knows all things."*

-1 John 3:20

———

*"There is therefore now no condemnation,*
*for those that are in Christ Jesus."*

-Romans 8:1

We are forgiven, and have been cleansed! In some mysterious way that we do not really understand, we are becoming partakers of the divine nature, allowing us to escape the world's corruption and evil desires.

S.G. Preston

**Peace Be With You**

Condemnation has been banished, replaced by the Holy Spirit with the peace of God.  As our Lord tells us:

*"Peace I leave with you, My peace I give you;*
*not as the world gives, do I give to you.*

*Let not your heart be troubled,*
*neither let it be afraid."*

-John 14:27

———

*"And the peace of God,*
*which passes all understanding,*
*shall keep your hearts and minds*
*through Christ Jesus."*

-Philippians 4:7

85

# 2.10  Lay Monks: Consecrated Christians

*"Meditation is the activity of calling to mind,*
*and thinking over, and dwelling on,*
*and applying to oneself,*
*the various things that one knows*
*about the works and ways and purposes*
*and promises of God.*

*It is an activity of holy thought,*
*consciously performed*
*in the presence of God, under the eye of God,*
*by the help of God,*
*as a means of communion with God.*

-J.I. Packer (1926-2020) Author: *Knowing God*

## Abiding in Christ

I begin my prayer at first awaking by making the Sign of the Cross, while praying:

*"In the Name of the Father, and of the Son,*
*and of the Holy Spirit.  Amen."*

-Matthew 28:19

Followed by:

*"This is the day that the Lord has made.*
*We will rejoice and be glad in it!*

-Psalm 118:24

Next, I may pray either Psalm 5, or *St. Patrick's Breastplate Prayer*, or what I have chosen to call *The Nine Affirmations*, depending on the day.

I will pray the *Nicene Creed* sometime during the day, every day, and on some days, I choose it to be my Awaking Prayer. We have committed all of these to memory, but of course you could also pray them as you read them.

## Tabula Rasa

Finally, I will consecrate myself to the Lord for this new day that God has given me, a *tabula rasa*: a new, clean slate. Every new day is a wonderful gift from God, in which we can start over and begin again, because the Lord's mercies and compassions:

*"... are new every morning."*

-Lamentations 3:23

Under the Old Covenant, when the Law was given to the people, they were asked to consecrate themselves to the LORD, so that they might receive a blessing:

*"Consecrate yourselves today to the LORD...*
*that He may bestow upon you a blessing this day."*

-Exodus 22:39

How much more then, should we who are under the New Covenant of Grace consecrate ourselves to God?

## Knowing Christ

The essence of Christianity consists simply of knowing Christ as our personal Lord and Savior. The Bible teaches:

*"But as many as received Him,*
*to them He gave power*
*to become the sons and daughters of God.*

-John 1:14

**Abiding In Christ**

Our Lord said:

> *"Abide in me, and I in you.*
> *As the branch cannot bear fruit of itself,*
> *unless it abides in the vine,*
> *neither can you,*
> *unless you abide in me."*

-John 15:3-5

The essence of prayer is communion with our Creator. It is abiding in Christ. Then what, to us, is the ultimate essence of our practice of *Celtic New Monasticism?*

What do we mean when we say that we are *Celtic Lay Monks?*

> *"All we really mean by being a "Lay Monk"*
> *is to be a consecrated Christian,*
> *especially devoted to prayer and to God's Word."*

-Based on Acts 6:4

It is my hope and prayer that all Christians might become such *"lay monks."*

**The Sign of the Cross**

I extinguish the candle that I had lighted earlier, and as I leave the Chapel, I again make the Sign of the Cross, once more praying:

> *"In the Name of the Father, and of the Son,*
> *and of the Holy Spirit. Amen."*

Why would an Evangelical make the Sign of the Cross? Because it was the practice of the Early Church?

88

It is a conscious act to dedicate our actions to God. If we cannot dedicate whatever we are doing to the Lord, we probably shouldn't be doing it at all.

There are so many additional reasons for making the Sign of the Cross that most Evangelicals are unaware of, that a small book would be necessary to explain them all.

It just so happens that there are several such small books.

## The Early Church

One that I was blessed by is *The Sign of the Cross: The Gesture, the Mystery, the History* by Andreas Andreopoulos, an Orthodox Priest. I read it out of curiosity. It did not convince me to make the Sign of the Cross, because I was already doing that, following the example of the Early Church.

But why *wouldn't* an Evangelical Christian make the Sign of the Cross? Of course, with our freedom in Christ we are equally free to do so, or not to do so.

You may be thinking: because most Evangelicals consider it to be an exclusively Roman Catholic practice. In fact, it is also an Eastern Orthodox practice. Among Protestants, it is an Anglican Practice, and a Lutheran practice.

All of these Churches received this practice, handed down to them from the Early Church; none of them originated it.

## 201 A.D.: The Early Church On Making The Sign of the Cross

In Chapter 3 of his *De Corona*, written c. 201 A.D., Tertullian calls making the Sign of the Cross an *ancient* practice! One does not call something an ancient practice if it was begun in your own lifetime, and Tertullian was born between 160 and 170 A.D.

To put this in perspective, remember that the Apostle John was still alive and Bishop of Ephesus until sometime after 98 A.D. It is generally believed that he died c. 100 A.D., at the age of 93 or 94: only 60 or 70 years before Tertullian was born.

## De Corona

Tertullian wrote (Boldface mine):

*"And how long shall we draw the saw to and fro through this line,
when we have **an ancient practice**,
which by anticipation has made for us the state, i.e., of the
question?*

*If no passage of Scripture has prescribed it,
assuredly custom, which without doubt flowed from tradition,
has confirmed it.*

*For how can anything come into use,
if it has not first **been handed down?***

*...At every forward step and movement,
at every going in an out,
when we put on our clothes and shoes,
when we bathe, when we sit at table,
when we light the lamps, on couch, on seat,*

*in all the ordinary actions of daily life,
**we trace upon the forehead the sign**."*

## A Capital Crime

The Early Church made the Sign of the Cross with their thumb on their forehead, so as not to be too conspicuous. It was a *sign* that you were a Christian, and Christianity was illegal in the Roman Empire.

Being a Christian was a capital crime, punishable by death, although this law might be enforced only during times of persecution.

There would be intermittent persecutions for another 100 years after Tertullian wrote the words quoted above, until Christianity was made legal for the first time in 313 A.D., by the Roman Emperor Constantine.

S.G. Preston

Open worship was finally allowed, and churches were built. Christians began making the Sign of the Cross with the larger motions still in use today.

Christians now, for the first time, safely *could* make the Sign, and *it became a witness* to non-Christians, as well as other Christians, that they belonged to Christ.

## A Protestant Practice

You may have been surprised to learn that making the Sign of the Cross has been a Protestant practice from the very beginning of Protestantism.

As I have pointed out, it has *always* been practiced in the Anglican Church, throughout the world.

## 1529: Martin Luther and The Sign of the Cross

And what about Martin Luther? If Luther was not a *Protestant*, who was?

Luther, in his *Small Catechism*, which he himself considered to be the best and most important thing that he ever wrote, and which is still used in Lutheran Churches today, suggested that the head of the household should teach his entire family to begin Morning and Evening Prayers in this way:

*"In the morning, when you get up,*
*make the sign of the cross and say:*

*'In the Name of the Father*
*and of the Son*
*and of the Holy Spirit.*
*Amen.'"*

Luther recommended following this with the *Apostle's Creed* and the *Lord's Prayer*. In many Lutheran Churches the *Apostles Creed* is alternated every other Sunday with the *Nicene Creed*.

**This Is the Day...**

Throughout the day, as I stand or kneel for prayer, I will give thanks and praise to the LORD for this day...

*"...that the LORD has made."*

Is not the gift of every new day a wonderful blessing? Let us then:

*"...rejoice and be glad in it."*

*"I Ainm an Athar, agus a Mhic,
agus an Spioraid Naoimh. Amen.*

*"In the Name of the Father, and of the Son,
and of the Holy Spirit. Amen."*

\* \* \*

S.G. Preston

## Christ Our Intercessor:

*"Cast all your cares upon Him, for He cares for you."*
(1 Peter 5:7)

*"Having therefore boldness to enter into the Holy of Holies by the blood of Jesus:* (Hebrews 10:19)

*"Let us then go boldly to the throne of grace, so that we can receive mercy, and find grace to help in time of need."*
(Hebrews 4:16)

*"Therefore He is able to save those to the uttermost those that draw near to God through Him, seeing He ever lives to make intercession for them."* (Hebrews 7:25)

*"For Christ has not entered into the holy places made with hands, which are only copies of the true one; but into heaven itself; now to appear in the presence of God for us…"* (Hebrews 9:24)

*"My little children, these things I write to you, so that you do not sin. But if anyone sins, we have an advocate with the Father, Jesus Christ the righteous: He is the propitiation for our sins; and not for ours only, but also for the sins of the whole world."*
(1 John 2:2)

*"I pray for them: I do not pray for the world, but for those that You have given to me, for they are yours."* (John 17:9)

*"I do not pray that You should take them out of the world, but that You should keep them from the evil."* (John 17:15)

*"Who is he that that condemns? It is Christ that died, yes rather, that is risen, who is even at the right hand of God, who also makes intercession for us."* (Romans 8:34)

*"If God is for us, who can be against us."* (Romans 8:31)

\* \* \*

# *Answers to Prayer*
## *PrayerFoundation™ 24-Hr. Prayerchain*

### Sept. 19, 2003 - Prayer Request:

Please pray for Tom. He broke his arm six months ago, and it is not healing. His Doctor says they will have to perform surgery.

*-Robert (Washington State)*

### Oct. 9, 2003 - Answer to Prayer:

Keep praying for Tom's arm, which had not been healing from a break for over six months, but began healing when your *Prayerchain* began praying for him. Thanks so much.

*-Robert (Washington State)*

### Oct. 17, 2003 - Answer to Prayer Update:

The Doctors said Tom still needed surgery, because his arm was only ten percent healed. When Tom went in for his surgery, they did a preliminary X-ray, and his Doctor was shocked, because the arm was 80% healed! The Surgeon canceled Tom's surgery, saying it was no longer necessary! Tom's healing is truly a miracle! Thank you so much, all of you who were praying.

*-Robert (Washington State)*

---

(From the book: *Answers to Prayer* by S.G. Preston)

# 3: *A Life of "Prayer Without Ceasing"*

## 3.1 Dedicating a Daily Hour to Prayer

*"Abba Arsenius*
*once asked an older monk from Egypt*
*for advice about*
*all of his temptations.*

*Another monk saw him doing this,*
*and said, 'Abba Arsenius,*
*how can it be*
*that you are so learned*
*in the Latin and Greek languages,*
*yet you ask a peasant*
*with no education*
*concerning your temptations?'*

*Monk Arsenius answered,*
*'I have great worldly knowledge*
*of Latin and Greek,*
*but I still have not been successful*
*in even learning the alphabet*
*of this peasant.'"*

-Sayings of the Desert Fathers

**Receiving Christ**

Growing up in the Midwest, I was born and raised beside Lake Michigan in Racine, Wisconsin. It is located along the lakeshore between Milwaukee and Chicago, about 35 minutes south of Milwaukee.

I have already told how, at the age of nineteen, I became a Christian. It was just one month short of my twentieth birthday.

## Go and Sell All That You Have

Four months later, I gave away everything I owned, and went out sharing my faith at my former High School, not knowing where I would sleep that night, and not worried about it at all.

I was excited by the idea of "living on faith."

God provided a place for me that night, and over the next four years, I practiced one-on-one witnessing on the street, and ministered at Church and public evangelism rallies in the Midwest, the eastern half of the United States, and Canada.

All this time I was devouring every book on prayer I could find, but was especially motivated to pray by the inspiring works of E.M. Bounds, and in particular by his book: *Power Through Prayer.*

## Visiting the Rockies

Back in the Midwest, I went on vacation to the Rocky Mountains in western Montana. The nearest mountain range was located on the border between eastern Idaho and the beautiful Bitterroot Valley of Montana.

Never before having been in such an area, I hiked up into the Bitterroot Mountains. I found myself in an untouched wilderness, extending westward across the greater part of Idaho. There were seemingly unending forests of pine and fir as far as the eye could see.

Unpolluted creeks were filled with icy water from melting snow. These small streams were also filled with Brown, Cutthroat, and Rainbow Trout, and flowed down every mountain pass throughout the wilderness. Shallow rapids alternated with deeper pools formed by beaver dams.

## Prayer and Mountains

When my vacation ended, I returned to the Midwest, but three days later moved back out to the Rockies.

One of the nicest things about living near mountains, is that, like our Lord often did, you can:

> *"...go up onto a mountain to pray."*
>
> -Matthew 14:23

## Praying Psalms

I found myself often climbing mountains to pray. By this time, I had been setting aside an hour a day to pray for four years.

The first seven years that I prayed for an hour every day, I was blessed to have missed only three days.

When I prayed, I would primarily pray the Psalms. Memorizing them simultaneously as I prayed them, I would eventually arrive at the point where I could pray psalms for 2 1/2 hours without repeating any.

It takes about that long to pray fifty-eight psalms, if you pray them slowly and meditatively, at the same speed as if you were reading them. Although back then, I seldom prayed for more than an hour at a time.

I just prayed different psalms on different days. *Praying the Psalms has been a great blessing to me throughout my Christian life* (and yes, I will be repeating this many times, over and over again, throughout this book!).

## Prayer and National Parks

Spending much time in some of our wonderful National Parks: Yellowstone, Grand Teton, and Glacier; I enjoyed hiking, back-country camping, canoeing, horseback riding, swimming, and whitewater rafting.

Three summers in a row; and then once again many years later with Lay Monk Linda, I traveled north to camp in Banff and Jasper National Parks in the Canadian Rockies.

Often the days were so full, that there was seemingly no time to pray. This was solved by rising an hour before everyone else, even when tent camping.

I have many wonderful memories of times spent alone with God; praying in crisp, rain-dripping, evergreen forests at first light, on mountainsides in Canada.

**Samuel Chadwick's Prayer Truth:**

**God Manifests Himself to Those Who Pray in Secret**

Samuel Chadwick (1860-1932) wrote in his book, *The Path of Prayer*:

> *"He manifests Himself*
> *to those who pray in secret,*
> *as He cannot to those*
> *who have no inner sanctuary*
> *of the soul."*

# 3.2 Awareness of God's Presence

*"Maireann croí éadrom i bfad."*

*"A light heart lives long."*

-Old Gaelic Saying

———

*"A merry heart is like a good medicine..."*

-Proverbs 17:22

**Prayer and God's Presence**

The next step of growth in prayer that I would begin to practice, while not giving up my daily hour of prayer, was to attempt living in as continual awareness of the presence of God as possible.

I was learning from Brother Lawrence (c. 1614-1691), a 17th century Carmelite monk who worked as a cook in his monastery.

His spiritual practice was to always be aware of being in God's presence, as in a state of prayer; even while working all day in the kitchen with pots and pans, preparing food, or occasionally being out on the road, purchasing needed supplies for his monastery.

**In His Presence is Joy**

The Prophet Nehemiah exhorts us:

*"...the joy of the LORD is your strength."*

-Nehemiah 8:10

Through prayer, we enter into the Sanctuary in Heaven. By the blood of Christ we enter into the very presence of God, where we will obtain the joy of the Lord that is our strength:

*"Having therefore, brothers and sisters,*
*boldness to enter into the Holy of Holies*
*by the blood of Jesus…"*

-Hebrew 10:19

———

*"Let us therefore go boldly to the throne of grace."*

-Hebrews 4:16

———

*"…in Your presence is fullness of joy…"*

-Psalm 16:11

## Sensing God's Presence

The book that tells the story of Brother Lawrence and his prayer life, is *The Practice of the Presence of God.*

I read it over and over; eventually obtaining the audio version, and listening to it many times over the years. It records:

*"That his prayer was nothing else*
*but a sense of the presence of God,*

*his soul being at that time*
*insensible to everything but Divine love;*

*and that when the appointed times of prayer*
*were past,*
*he found no difference,*
*because he still continued with God,*

*praising and blessing Him with all his might,*
*so that he passed his life in continual joy.*

*Yet he hoped that God*
*would allow him some suffering,*
*that he should grow stronger.*

100

S.G. Preston

*That we ought to, once and for all,*
*heartily put our whole trust in God,*

*and make a total surrender of ourselves to Him,*
*secure that He would not deceive us."*

-Written about Brother Lawrence

## Prayer and Brother Lawrence

And this is Brother Lawrence himself, in his own words:

*"...when we are faithful to keep ourselves in His Holy Presence,*
*and set Him always before us;*

*this not only hinders our offending Him,*
*and doing anything that may displease Him,*
*at least willfully;*

*but it also begets in us a holy freedom...with God, by which we*
*ask, and successfully,*
*for the graces we stand in need of."*

-Brother Lawrence

## John Chrysostom and the Apostle Paul

We find the same teaching, 1,200 years earlier, in John
Chrysostom (347-407 A.D.), considered by Eastern Orthodoxy to be
one of the most important and influential Church Fathers:

*"There is nothing more worthwhile*
*than to pray to God and converse with Him,*
*for prayer unites us with God as His companions.*

*Even as our physical eyes are illuminated*
*by seeing the light,*
*so in contemplating God,*
*our soul is illuminated by Him.*

*Of course, the prayer I have in mind*
*is no matter of routine.*
*It is deliberate and earnest.*

*It is not tied to a fixed timetable.*
*Rather, it is a state*
*that endures night and day."*

The Apostle Paul taught that all people should seek the Lord, and find Him:

*"...He is not far from any one of us.*
*"For in Him we live, and move,*
*and have our being."*

-Acts 17:27-28

# 3.3 *"Pray Without Ceasing"*

*"'Pray without ceasing' has been the sentence repeating itself in my silent thoughts,*
*and I am sure that it will be, it must be,*
*my practice until the last conscious hour of my life.*

*Oh, why was it not my practice throughout that long, indolent, inanimate half century past!*
*I often think mournfully of the difference it would have made in me.*

*Now there remains so little time for a more genuine, effective spiritual life."*

-John Fletcher (1729-1785) Methodist
(Said on his deathbed.)

## Jesus Spoke a Parable

Brother Lawrence and John Chrysostom's teaching that the Christian life is continual prayer, of course is straight from the Bible:

*"Pray without ceasing."*

-1 Thessalonians 5:17

———

*"And Jesus spoke a parable to them, to teach them that they ought always to pray, and not to give up."*

-Luke 18:1

———

*"...we will devote ourselves continually to prayer..."*

-Acts 6:4

**My Meditation All Day Long**

> *"Seven times a day I praise You,*
> *because of Your righteous judgments."*

-Psalm 119:164

Seven in the Scriptures is the number used to signify completeness. In this verse from Psalm 119, as with the practice of the Apostles shown above in Acts 6:4, keeping our mind stayed on God is linked with keeping our minds stayed on *His Word.*

> *"The further the soul advances,*
> *the greater are the adversaries*
> *against which it must contend.*
>
> *Blessed are you,*
> *if the struggle grows fierce against you*
> *at the time of prayer.*
>
> *Do not allow your eyes to sleep,*
> *or your eyelids to slumber*
> *until the hour of your death;*
> *but labor without ceasing..."*

-Evagrius of Pontus (d. 399 A.D.)

**I Have Kept the LORD Always Before Me (Psalm 16:8)**

We also find this encouragement to keep our minds stayed on God's Word in other parts of the Bible:

> *"O, how I love Your law!*
> *It is my meditation all day long."*

-Psalm 119:97

——

> *"But His delight is in the law of the LORD,*

104

*and in His law,  He meditates day and night. "*

-Psalm 1:2


The wicked, on the other hand, are contrasted with God's people for *not* keeping their minds stayed on God:

*"The wicked, full of pride and arrogance,
will not seek after God.*

*God is not in any of their thoughts. "*

-Psalm 10:4

# 3.4 Evangelical Monasticism

*"Let a man set his heart only on doing the will of God and he is instantly free.*

*If we understand our first and sole duty to consist of loving God supremely and loving everyone, even our enemies, for God's dear sake,*

*then we can enjoy spiritual tranquility under every circumstance."*

-A.W. Tozer (1897-1963)
Pastor, Evangelist, Theologian
(Author, *The Knowledge of the Holy*)
Christian & Missionary Alliance

———

*"He who has learned to pray, has learned the greatest secret of a holy and a happy life."*

-William Law (1686-1761) Anglican Priest

## Becoming Monks

Earlier I told how in March of 1999, my wife Linda and I together felt led to Found the *PrayerFoundation* ™ ministry, and how we were the only Evangelical Christian monastics on the Internet until 2003.

Then, one by one, other evangelical monastic groups went online with their websites. Next, the floodgates opened!

By 2008, another five years later, there were over 100 groups calling themselves both *"monastic and Evangelical"* in North America alone, according to *The Boston Globe* (Feb. 23, 2008).

106

S.G. Preston

As of today, in 2018, there are now thousands of such groups worldwide.

## The Jesus Shema

Our Lord's summary of the greatest commandments: to love God, and love others, in Mark 12:29-31 is part of the Liturgy of our *Worship Service*.

It is used in both the Anglican and Roman Catholic Liturgies.

In the Anglican Book of Common Prayer, it has been referred to as *The Summary of the Law*. I refer to it as *The Jesus Shema*.

*The Shema*, or *Shema Yisrael*, begins the Morning and Nightly Jewish Prayer Service. *Shema* is a *Hebrew* word meaning: *Hear*. *Shema Yisrael* means: *Hear O Israel*:

*Shema Yisrael,
Adonai Eloheinu Adonai echad.*

*Hear O Israel,
the LORD our God, the LORD is one.*

-Deuteronomy 6:4

———

*"And Jesus answered,
'The first of all the commandments is:*

*'Hear O Israel,
the Lord our God, the Lord is one.*

*And you shall love the Lord your God
with all your heart,
and with all your soul,
and with all your mind,
and with all your strength.'*

*This is the first commandment.*

*And the second is like it, namely this:*

*'You shall love your neighbor as yourself.'*
*There is no other commandment greater than these."*

-Mark 12:29-31
Deuteronomy 6:4-5
Leviticus 19:18

## We Had Wanted to Be Monks Most of Our Lives

Lay Monk Linda and myself had always been interested in all things monastic. We had both wanted to be monks for most of our entire lives.

I had even looked into joining the Franciscan *Order of Friars Minor* at the age of sixteen, and was told I wasn't old enough, and would be required to convert to Roman Catholicism first.

I was not yet a born again Christian then: that is, I hadn't had a conversion experience and received Christ. I did, however, consider myself a Protestant, thinking that I had been "born one."

## Protestant Franciscan Orders

Yes, writing this now, it sounds very odd to me, too. Isn't *Protestant* supposed to be a *subset* of *Christian*?

In any case, I was Protestant enough to be less than enthused at the idea of converting to Roman Catholicism! I thought that this ruled out entirely for me the possibility of ever becoming a Franciscan.

In my ignorance, I was totally unaware that there had been Protestant Franciscan Orders in existence for over 160 years!

S.G. Preston

# 3.5 A *"Prayer Encouragement"* Ministry

*"Do not work so hard for Christ
that you have no strength to pray,
for prayer requires strength."*

-Hudson Taylor (1832-1905)
Founder: *China Inland Mission*

———

*"Prayer is the ascending vapor
which supplies the showers of blessing,
and the stream that flows
through earth's dry places,
till on every side,*

*'The wilderness shall blossom as the rose.'"*

-A.B. Simpson (1843-1919)
Founder: *Christian & Missionary Alliance* Church

**Founding a Prayer Ministry**

Linda and I had returned from our trip through Europe, deeply touched by visiting Assisi, the home of St. Francis, and ancient Celtic monastery sites in Ireland.

We felt that the time had finally arrived to found a prayer ministry of *"Prayer Encouragement"* with extensive *"Prayer Teaching & Resources from All Christian Communions & Eras."*

**Evangelical Monks**

It was a calling I had been feeling growing stronger for many, many years. Linda suggested that we also make it an *Evangelical Lay Monastic Order*. We had been studying the ancient Celtic monks ever since we had returned from Ireland, impressed by the fact that so many of them were *missionary monks*.

I had worked for years with different Evangelical Denominations and Non-Denominational Churches, and pointed out that the idea of *Evangelical Monks* would probably not be very well received by them.

## Hate Mail

Like Lay Monk Linda, my heart was for founding a monastic order of born again Celtic Lay Monks; but my concern was how this might affect, hurt, or hinder the prayer ministry that I also had a heart for.

Linda's belief was that if we were feeling led to found the very first born again Christian monastic Order, we should stand with the Apostles and the Word of God and *obey God, not men.* I agreed.

We did indeed receive *"hate mail"* for several years from some Protestants who did not like anything monastic, but now, eighteen years later, it has pretty much become a non-issue.

## Favorable Comments

On the other hand, the Protestants that we respect the most: *Pastors and Missionaries*; have written to us with very favorable comments regarding what we are doing.

We have also received such comments from Roman Catholic and Orthodox Monks, several Abbots of monasteries, some Hieromonks (Orthodox Monks who are Priests), many Bishops, an Archbishop, and even one Cardinal.

# 3.6 How We Pray

*"You will not see anyone who is truly striving after
his spiritual advancement
who is not given to spiritual reading."*

-Athanasius of Alexandria (c. 296/298–373 A.D.)

———

*"We read to know that we are not alone."*

-C.S. Lewis (1898-1963)

**Overview of Our Daily Prayer Life**

I am necessarily repeating here some of what I wrote earlier regarding my personal prayer practice.

Upon arising, we pray Psalm 5, or *The Nine Affirmations* or *St. Patrick's Breastplate Prayer*. The ancient Celtic monks began each day praying it. It is quite long; here is a small portion of it that you could begin praying every morning, if you would like to:

*"I arise today through a mighty strength,
the invocation of the Trinity,
through belief in the Threeness,
through confession of the Oneness,
of the Creator of creation."*

Most days I myself will pray all three. These are popular choices with us, but of course, anyone is free to pray however and whatever they prefer.

Now I know that some of you are saying, "I don't have the time...I already have to get up early! There is never enough time to sleep...I barely have time to brush my teeth before I have to go to work!"

I know you are saying these things because I have said them myself. If all you can pray is:

*"This is the day that the Lord has made.*
*We will rejoice and be glad in it!*

-Psalm 118:24

...you have already prayed more than many, if not most, of the people in this world.

### (An Aside) An Untypical Day: Once a Week

Every Saturday, ten months out of the year, for the past fourteen years, I have gotten up at 2:30 a.m., after only four or five hours of sleep.

I have a half hour drive to the craft market I make my living at (to me it is kind of like the Desert Fathers of Egypt weaving their reed baskets to support themselves) and I spend this time in prayer.

Arriving between 3:30 and 4 a.m., it takes me about three hours to move and set up my booth.

I will get another half hour of prayer in while I am doing this, most often memorized psalms, but about two and a half hours of that time I am too distracted, concentrating on what I doing, even to silently do this.

Sometimes I am able to sing hymns silently to myself.

But I have found that while I do this type of work, if I cannot concentrate enough to pray psalms or even sing Christian songs silently to myself, I can still be aware of God's presence: *I can practice the presence of God.*

### Prayer Time

Still, it is now only 6:30 a.m., and I have already prayed today for an hour. After driving home, I will get to sleep another hour and a half, have breakfast, and drive back for seven and a half hours more work at our booth.

Lay Monk Linda and I actually sell at the craft market two days a week, but I don't have to get up so early on the second day, because the booth has already been set up. Two hours total driving time all day, ten and a half hours working, and I will be all done and home by 6 p.m.

And yet I was still blessed to be able to fit in some prayer time.

## Like Daniel

Lay Monk Linda likes to pray *The Threefold Daily Prayers:* The Lord's Prayer, The 23rd Psalm, and Psalm 117 all in a row, the first thing after awaking.

She does this in case she either forgets, or is later doing something that prevents praying them at their three specific times, although most likely she will pray each of them again at those times.

After awaking, she always prays kneeling in front of a low second story window *"Like Daniel,"* as she says. The sill is only about eight inches above the floor.

## 7 a.m.

## Back to a Typical Day: A Little Later We Will Spend an Hour in Personal, Private Prayer:

During which we will often pray several more psalms that we have committed to memory. This is a good time to pray *the minimum one psalm,* or *five psalms a day,* or whatever we have chosen to observe currently as a spiritual discipline.

Sometimes I will pray the entire Liturgy of our *Worship Service*; which takes about an hour, after leaving out the Scripture Readings, Hymns, and Christian Teaching (yes, I memorized it; it is almost 100% Scripture). Other times I will just worship in a silent attitude of prayer for part of, or for the entire hour.

**The Three New Testament Prayer Times: 9 a.m., Noon, 3 p.m.**

As mentioned above, we observe what I have chosen to call the *Threefold Daily Prayers*: (9a.m., Noon, and 3p.m.).

Our Order prays *The Lord's Prayer, The 23rd Psalm*, and *Psalm 117* respectively, at these three special historical times for Christian prayer.

We will take a good look at the example of the Apostles in the New Testament and the testimony of the Early Church regarding this ancient Biblical prayer practice, in my book: *Prayer as a Celtic Lay Monk.*

It was observed by all Christians up through the 800's A.D.

At that time, like so many of the Early Church's Christian spiritual practices, including the praying of the Psalms, it was relegated to the monasteries, where it has been continuously observed to this very day.

(Scripture References for the common prayer times of the Apostles and the Early Church: Psalm 55:17; Daniel 6:10; Matthew 15:36; Luke 18:10; Acts 2:15, 3:1, 10:3,9; 10:30; 16:25; 27:35).

*"Touching the time, however,*
*the extrinsic observance*
*of certain hours*
*will not be unprofitable –*

*those common hours, I mean,*
*which mark the intervals of the day --*
*the third, the sixth, the ninth –*

*which we may find in the Scriptures*
*to have been more solemn*
*than the rest."*

-Tertullian, c. 200 A.D.
Writing in *"On Prayer"* (Chapter 25)

S.G. Preston

**Spontaneous Prayer is Offered By Everyone Through the Day**

We also pray at meals, of course. And pray for safety when anyone leaves the monastery, including our dog and cats…and give thanks upon their return.

We think our thoughts to God…and try to be aware of being in His presence all day long.

Does this sound burdensome? Is it burdensome to have to breathe all day long? To us it does not seem to be a burden at all. It is just our way of life.

**(About) 6 p.m.**

**Family Chapel:**

Lay Monk Linda and I have long had the practice of getting together in our monastery Chapel for 15 minutes (or more) of Family Prayer together in the evening.

**(About) 9 p.m.**

**Before Sleep**

Either silently individually, or out loud together, we either pray the Franciscan prayer, *Lord, Make Me an Instrument of Thy Peace*, or Psalm 4, or both.

We may continue praying together, or pray silently and individually, for another 15 minutes, or up to an hour; until we are sleepy.

**Midnight Prayer:**

If we wake up in the middle of the night, we sing Psalm 134, and pray the Midnight Prayer (Psalm 119:62):

> *"At midnight I will rise to give thanks to You, because of your righteous judgements."*

**Spiritual Reading:**

We observe daily Scripture reading.

We read Christian Books *as able,* fifteen minutes here and there, sometimes during meals. Over 200 of the very best have been collected by us. They were all reviewed on our original website.

(Note: *"...as able,"* This applies to everything. We do what we can, when we can.

No one can do everything all of the time, nor does God expect anyone to. Trying to do so would be to fall into legalism, leading to condemnation, which Scripture teaches us is never from God. See: Romans 8:1).

This is a very common mistake, one that C.S. Lewis recalled Blaise Pascal pointing out:

> *"...what Pascal, if I remember rightly,*
> *calls 'Error of Stoicism':*
>
> *thinking we can do always*
> *what we can do sometimes."*

**Christian History Magazine**

Our favorite magazine is: *Christian History Magazine.* A quarterly magazine, published four times a year by the same ministry, *Vision Video,* through which we obtained our collection of excellent Christian Films.

It has been a joy to read every new issue, over several decades now. Each magazine provides a learning experience, one that is very inspiring.

We collect them, save them, and re-read them. We are missing only four out of over 125 issues.

Myself and Lay Monk Bob especially have greatly enjoyed and benefitted from reading them.

S.G. Preston

**Spiritual Listening:**

In the car, while doing errands (two hours a day?), beginning in January:

The entire Bible – takes about 3 months; a different version each year.

Dr. J. Vernon McGee's 5-year *Thru the Bible* Program – also takes about 3 months.

Christian Audiobooks we own, and from the Public Library – the rest of the year.

I followed the practice listed above for five years. Now…*as able.*

**Christian Film Night:**

Once a week we have a Christian Film Night. We have collected over 200 Christian Films. They were all reviewed on our original website.

We have often stopped the film to discuss it; a half-hour video may take an hour to watch. A two-hour film will often be watched over four hours, half each week over two weeks.

In this way we were able to have great fellowship with Lay Monk Bob, and with other believers, as when a Christian individual or group would visit to watch a film with us.

**Worship Service**

We follow the Film with our *Worship Service.* If it includes Hymns and Scripture Readings, it lasts an hour and a half. With Christian Teaching: two hours.

It is a formal Liturgical Service, assembled and edited by myself over many decades of research and study, based on the most ancient Liturgies, It is essentially a third century worship service; compared with Scripture, and consisting almost exclusively of Scripture.

117

These are the earliest recorded written Worship Service Liturgies that we have. Christianity was a Capital crime, punishable by death, until the Emperor Constantine legalized it in 313 A.D. Services were memorized, and generally not written down, to avoid their use as evidence in persecution.

Our Liturgy has seemed familiar to visiting Lutherans, Anglicans, Presbyterians, and Roman Catholics. Every Service includes Communion, preceded by the *Nicene Creed*, which is itself a compilation of Scripture.

We have been using the Liturgy of our *Worship Service* for nineteen years as of this writing (2018).

It always feels too short, and over too soon.

# 3.7  Desiring a Deeper Prayer Life

*"O Master carpenter,*
*who at the last through wood and nails,*
*did purchase man's whole salvation:*

*wield well Thy tools in this Thy workshop,*
*so that we who come to Thee rough-hewn,*
*may by Thy grace,*
*be fashioned into a nobler beauty.  Amen."*

-The Hillcroft Prayer (Celtic)

**Your Comments**

Because our website is viewed by so many people throughout the world, we receive a *lot* of emails.  We receive many more emails than we could ever possibly answer, but we answer those we can.

Some, like the one shown here, reflect a concern felt by many Christians.

**An Email We Received:**

*"I want to grow in my prayer life,*
*but I'm not sure how.*
*I have prayed that God will show me what to do.*

*I have a list of people that I pray for about various things (healing, salvation, a job, etc.).*
*I feel that I pray the same thing every day.*

*I want more in my prayers for these people*
*and for both myself and my family.*

*Please let me know what I can do to make my prayers more heartfelt (sometimes I feel I'm just reciting them).*

*I do talk to God throughout the day*

*and express my feelings to Him on a daily basis, but it's not in*
*prayer form.*
*It's more like just talking to someone in the room.*
*But I still want a better prayer life."*

**My Reply:**

We also have always desired a deeper prayer life. The answer to your question is something that we have dedicated our lives to answering, and is the entire purpose of our ministry and most aspects of what we do every day, all day long.

You have requested some practical advice. We think that prayer is an individual matter, and that the Lord leads everyone uniquely. Here are some suggestions, offered in the hope that one or more of them may be of help to you:

You have said that you have prayed that God will show you what to do.

*That is the first and best*
*answer to your question.*

In the next Section, we will look at *Nine Ways to Pray* that we have found to be helpful in our own prayer lives.

S.G. Preston

# 3.8 Nine Ways to Pray

*"Distractions must be conquered
or they will conquer us.
So let us cultivate simplicity."*

*"I think that some of the greatest prayer
is prayer where you don't say one single word
or ask for anything."*

*"Prayer is always in danger
of degenerating into a glorified gold rush.*

*How to get things from God
occupies most (books)."*

-A.W. Tozer (1897-1963)
Christian & Missionary Alliance
Author: *"The Knowledge of the Holy"*

**A Personal Prayer Tip:**

**Nine Ways to Pray**

**C**onfession, Supplication, Intercession
Praise, Thanksgiving, Silence,
Adoration, Scripture Memorization, Meditation On the
Word of God

*"There is not in the world
a kind of life
more sweet and delightful,
than that of a continual conversation
with God;
those only can comprehend it
who practice
and experience it."*

-Brother Lawrence

*We think that you are doing much better than you realize.* We do not recognize any particular *"form"* of prayer as being exclusively the one correct way to pray. Here are nine ways to pray that have helped us draw closer to God in our prayer lives. I do not mean to imply that there are *only* nine ways!

Your *"talking to God"* in prayer all day long is no less valid prayer than any other kind at any other time. *We do the same.* Prayer is both communion and communication with God.

We talk with God at specific times set aside for prayer. We also *practice the presence of God* and *"pray without ceasing"* when we think our thoughts all day to God during the day.

## Confession:

…of our sins is followed by asking for and receiving forgiveness:

*"If we **confess** our sins,*
*He is faithful and just to forgive us our sins,*
*and to cleanse us from all unrighteousness."*

-1 John 1:9

———

*"The confession of evil works*
*is the first beginning of good works."*

-St. Augustine of Hippo

## Supplication:

Is making a *petition* (asking for something) for yourself or for others.

*"The great thing in prayer is to feel that we are putting*
*our **supplications** into the bosom of omnipotent love."*

-Andrew Murray

122

S.G. Preston

**Intercession:**

Is *supplication* for others.

*"Prayer must be broad in its scope –*
*it must plead for others.*

***Intercession*** *for others is the hallmark of all true prayer.*

*When prayer is confined to self*
*and to the sphere of one's personal needs,*

*it dies by reason of littleness,*
*narrowness and selfishness. "*

-E.M. Bounds

We who have received Christ as our Lord and Savior, have been given the office of priest and prophet. Each of us has been individually chosen and ordained for this by Christ Himself.

Our office of prophet is to give out the Word of God to the world. This is the Lord's command in His *Great Commission* (Mark 16:15).

Our office of priest (*"But you are a...royal priesthood..."* -1 Peter 2:9) is to **intercede** in prayer for all people.

*"I urge therefore, that, first of all,*
*supplications, prayers,* ***intercessions,***
*and giving of thanks,*
*be made for all people..."*

-1 Timothy 2:1

As Christians, it is who we are. It is what we do. It is our calling in Christ.

*"...for You were slain,*
*and have redeemed us to God by Your blood*
*out of every tribe, and language, and people, and nation;*

123

*and have made us unto our God*
*kings and priests…"*

-Revelation 5:9-10

———

*"You have not chosen Me,*
*but I have chosen you, and ordained you,*

*that you should go and bring forth fruit,*
*and that your fruit should remain:*

*that whatever you shall ask of the Father*
*in My name, He will give it to you."*

-John 15:16

**Praise:**

*"O **praise** the LORD all ye nations,*
***praise** him, all ye people.*

*For His merciful kindness is great toward us,*
*and the truth of the Lord endureth forever.*

***Praise** ye the LORD!"*

-Psalm 117

This is the complete text of Psalm 117, only two verses long, which we pray every day.

**Thanksgiving:**

Is giving glory to God. Our Lord healed ten lepers, but only one returned to thank him:

*"And Jesus answering said,*
*'Were not ten cleansed?*
*But where are the nine?*

124

S.G. Preston

*There are not any found
that returned to **give glory to God**,
except this stranger...* "

-Luke 17:17-18

*"There should be a parallel between
our supplications and our **thanksgivings**.*

*We ought not to leap in prayer,
and limp in praise. "*

-Charles Spurgeon

**Silence:**

*"In prayer it is better to have
a heart without words
than words without a heart. "*

-John Bunyan

Prayer can also be simply sitting in *silence* in His presence. These verses are recited before the part of our *Worship Service* where we wait in silence upon the Lord (between two bell rings):

*"...the LORD is in His Holy Temple.
Let all the earth keep **silence** before Him... "*

-Habakkuk 2:20

———

*"**Be still**, and know that I am God.
I will be exalted among the nations.
I will be exalted in the earth. "*

-Psalm 46:10

———

125

*"There come times when I have nothing more to tell God.*
*If I were to continue to pray in words,*
*I would have to repeat what I have already said.*
*At such times it is wonderful to say to God, '*
*May I be in Thy presence, Lord?*
*I have nothing more to say to Thee,*
*but I do love to be in Thy presence.'"*

-O. Hallesby  (Author of the book: *Prayer*)

## Adoration:

…can be expressed silently or verbally.

*"Prayer is either a sheer illusion or a personal contact between*
*embryonic, incomplete persons (ourselves)*
*and the utterly concrete Person.*
*Prayer in the sense of petition, asking for things,*
*is a small part of it;*
*confession and penitence are its threshold, **adoration** its sanctuary,*
*the presence and vision and enjoyment of God its bread and wine.*
*In it God shows Himself to us."*

-C.S. Lewis

## Meditation On the Word of God:

*Give ear to my words, O LORD,*
*consider my meditation.*
*Hear the sound of my cry, my King and my God,*
*for unto You I will pray."*

-Psalm 5:1-2

———

*"My meditation Him shall be sweet:*
*I will be glad in the LORD."*

-Psalm 104:34

126

———

*"I remember the days of old;*
*I meditate on all that you have done,*
*I ponder the work of your hands."*

-Psalm 143:5

———

*"My hands also will I lift up*
*unto Your commandments, which I have loved;*
*and I will meditate on Your statutes."*

-Psalm 119:48

———

*"My eyes are awake before the night watches,*
*that I may meditate on your word."*

-Psalm 119:148

———

*"I have more understanding than all my teachers, for Your*
*testimonies are my meditation."*

-Psalm 119:99

Scripture Meditation can done as a separate prayer practice, or it can be combined with the use of Scripture Memorization in prayer.

## Scripture Memorization:

Is a most wonderful way to pray. What both Athanasius and Martin Luther said about praying the Psalms (God's Prayer Book) applies here too: *that God is speaking to us at the same time that we are speaking to Him.*

*"I will meditate on Your precepts,*
*and have respect unto Your ways."*

127

*I will delight in your statutes;*
*I will not forget Your word."*

-Psalm 119:15-16

----

*"The law of God is in his heart:*
*none of his steps shall slide."*

-Psalm 37:31

----

*"I have hidden Your word in my heart,*
*that I might not sin against you."*

-Psalm 119:11

----

*"Let the word of Christ dwell in you richly..."*

-Colossians 3:16

**A Personal Prayer Tip:**

**Prayer is More Than Asking for Things, Including Help**

Many Christians who are bored with their prayer lives, often seem to be laboring under a great misunderstanding about prayer.

It is as though they think that prayer consists *solely* of **petition** and **supplication** (asking for things): just presenting God with a "laundry list" of requests.

It is not surprising that they find this boring, and run out of things to ask for when they would like to pray longer.

As a new Christian, when I began dedicating an hour a day to prayer, I had the same problem. I solved it this way: during an hour of prayer, I seldom pray for more than five or ten minutes "asking for things" (*petition* and *supplication*). Then I move on to other types of prayer: communion and communication through worship:

S.G. Preston

### *Praise, Adoration, Confession, Silence,*
### *Scripture Memorization,*
### *Meditation On the Word of God*

Another self-caused problem comes from the natural, but wrong, tendency to go to the Lord when we have a problem and then forget about the Lord when it is solved, when we don't *"need"* him anymore.

This is how we acted in our old lives, before we became Christians. Now we know that we *need* the Lord at all times!

**An Andrew Murray Prayer Tip:**

**Prayer is Abiding in Christ**

Andrew Murray (1828-1917), a Dutch Reformed Pastor in South Africa, stated it this way in his excellent book, *With Christ in the School of Prayer:*

> *"Christ teaches us to pray not only by example,*
> *by instruction, by command, by promises;*
> *but by showing us Himself,*
> *the ever-living intercessor, as our Life.*
>
> *It is when we believe this,*
> *and go and abide in Him for our prayer-life too,*
> *that our fears of not being able to pray aright*
> *will vanish;*
>
> *and we shall joyfully and triumphantly*
> *trust our Lord to teach us to pray,*
> *to be Himself the life and power of our prayer."*

\* \* \*

## *Answers to Prayer*
### *PrayerFoundation™ 24-Hr. Prayerchain*

### Nov. 18, 2005 - Prayer Request:

Please pray for the believers in the Himachal Pradesh region of India. A group of radical Hindus have beaten a pastor, and threatened to burn more than 60 new converts to death if they do not re-convert to Hinduism. This area is home to a large shrine to the Hindu "god" Shiva, and since the tourist visits are so important to the local economy, the police are dragging their feet in becoming involved. Please pray for the protection of the believers, and pray that the hearts of the attackers would be softened to the Gospel. Thank you again for praying,

*-Brother Seamus (Ontario, Canada)*

### Answer to Prayer - Nov. 27, 2005

Bless God! The plan to kill believers in Himachal Pradesh, India if they did not reconvert to Hinduism has been thwarted. The date set was Sunday the 20th of November. The only ceremony that day was *church!* And the police, who had been trying to stay uninvolved, actually met with the Hindu community (including the media!) and explained that Christian conversion was one of choice, and that the new believers had not been coerced.

They told the people that those who had been speaking against the church were misleading them. The pastor's son said that they met without incident.

*-Brother Seamus (Ontario, Canada)*

---

(From the book: *Answers to Prayer* by S.G. Preston)

# 4: *Great Lives of Prayer in History*

## 4.1 Heroes of Faith

*"A monk had done something wrong.*
*Abba Moses was called for*
*by a meeting of Elders,*
*and was asked to join them.*

*Monk Moses did not want to.*

*A message was delivered from a Priest,*
*saying, 'Please come,*
*the entire community*
*of Brothers is assembled here*
*and awaiting your arrival.'*

*Moses still did not wish to go, but he went anyway.*
*Monk Moses obtained an old basket*
*made of woven reeds.*
*It was filled with holes.*
*Filling the basket to the brim with sand,*
*he dragged it along behind him as he walked.*

*'Abba Moses, what is this?'*
*the Elders asked, when he arrived.*
*Moses answered,*
*'My sins are all streaming out behind me,*
*but I am totally unaware of any of them.*
*And yet today you have invited me here*
*to judge another's sins!'*

*After listening to these words of Abba Moses,*
*the Elders pardoned the Brother*
*and decided to forget the entire affair."*

-Sayings of the Desert Fathers

131

## Great Lives of Prayer Inspire Us

Christian biographies have been *sanctioned* (approved) by God for our edification and growth in Christ.

He has shown us this, by using them in his listing of the biblical *heroes of faith* in the eleventh chapter of the book of Hebrews, and by the very recording in Holy Scripture of the lives of the Old Testament saints. God's Word states:

> *"Now all these things happened to them*
> *for our example,*
> *and they are written for our instruction..."*
>
> -1 Corinthians 10:11

So many great lives of prayer! The Bible is filled with them:

> *Abraham, Joseph,*
> *Moses, David, Daniel,*
> *Elijah, Isaiah, and Jeremiah*
> *in the Old Testament.*
>
> *Christ and the Apostles*
> *in the New Testament.*

We are familiar with these and many others from the pages of Scripture.

## Great Men and Women of Prayer Teach Us Much

But what of all the Christians who have lived *since* the days of the New Testament? How many of these were great saints of prayer? More than can ever be mentioned in any one book.

Many who are well known, and many, many more that we will not learn about, until we join them with our Lord in Heaven.

Our ministry has spent much time studying and learning from past great men and women of prayer. Truly it is said of we who are Christians today, that we *"stand on the shoulders of giants."*

They are so numerous that we can do little more than briefly list a very few of those who have had the most influence on our own lives.

## Heroes of the Faith

Eastern Orthodox and Roman Catholics may find it somewhat strange that many Protestants do not seem to acknowledge certain Christians as *"saints,"* *although in fact they do.*

Both views are held simultaneously, because of the Protestant belief that the Scriptures refer to *all* believing Christians as *saints.*

*"A rose by any other name..."*

-William Shakespeare (1564-1616 )
Romeo & Juliet: Act II, Scene II

But the basic underlying idea, that there are certain Christians that are especially spiritual, lead lives greatly inspiring, and have a closer walk with the Lord, *is* acknowledged. Protestants just call them by different, unofficial terms:

*Great Christians,*
*Heroes of the Faith,*
*Great Prayer Lives,*
*Great Saints of Prayer,*
*and other names.*

# 4.2  Great Saints of Prayer

*"I have read the lives of many eminent Christians
who have been on earth since the Bible days.*

*Some of them, I see, were rich, and some poor.
Some were learned, and some unlearned.*

*Some of them were Episcopalians, and some Christians of other
names.
Some were Calvinists, and some were Arminians.
Some have loved to use a liturgy,
and some to use none.*

*But one thing I see, they all had in common.
They have all been men of prayer."*

-Bishop J.C. Ryle
Anglican (1816-1900)

———

*"Cuimhnichibh air na daoine
bho'n dthainig tú sibh."*

*"Remember the people who you come from."*

-Old Gaelic Saying

## Early Church Era

**P**olycarp, Perpetua, Irenaeus of Lyon,
Anthony of Egypt, Pachomius of Egypt,
The Desert Fathers, The Desert Mothers,
*Athanasius of Alexandria, Basil the Great,
Gregory of Nyssa, Gregory of Nazianzus,
Ambrose of Milan, Augustine of Hippo,
John Cassian, Evagrius of Pontus,
John Chrysostom, Maximus the Confessor,
John Climacus, Martin of Tours.*

S.G. Preston

## Celtic Christian Era

*Ninian of Caledonia, Patrick of Ireland,*
*Brigid of Kildare, Ita of Killeedy,*
*Brendan the Navigator, Kevin of Glendalough,*
*Columba of Iona, Aidan of Lindisfarne,*
*Hilda of Whitby, Cuthbert of Lindisfarne,*
*Columbanus of Leinster, David of Wales,*
*Samson of Wales, The Venerable Bede.*

## Medieval Era

*Benedict of Nursia, Gregory the Great,*
*Bernard of Clairvaux, Francis of Assisi,*
*John Wycliffe, Jan Hus.*

## Reformation Era

*Martin Luther, John Calvin,*
*Ulrich Zwingli. William Tyndale,*
*Archbishop Cranmer, Menno Simons,*
*John Knox, August Francke.*

## Colonial Era

*George Fox, Brother Lawrence, Count Zinzendorf,*
*David Brainerd, Jonathan Edwards,*
*John Wesley, George Whitefield,*
*John Newton, William Wilberforce.*

## World Missions Era

*William Carey, Edward Payson, Adoniram Judson,*
*John Payton, Robert Murray M'Cheyne, Bishop J.C. Ryle,*
*E.M. Bounds, Andrew Murray, Charles Spurgeon,*
*George Müller, Hudson Taylor, Dwight Moody,*
*A.B. Simpson, William and Catherine Booth.*

## Modern Era

*R.A. Torrey, Amy Carmichael, O. Hallesby,*
*A.W. Tozer, C.S. Lewis, Corrie ten Boom,*
*Francis and Edith Schaeffer, Bill Bright,*
*Ken Curtis, J.I. Packer, Billy Graham.*

(Note: I have not included anyone not yet called home to be with the Lord on the list for the Modern Era, though several people come to mind.)

## An Andrew Murray Prayer Tip:

## The Necessity of Godliness to Have an Effective Prayer Life

We learned much about the different types of Biblical prayer from Andrew Murray in his classic book: *"With Christ in the School of Prayer."*

Murray stresses the necessity of holiness and godliness, if we would be effective men and women of prayer. For those of us with past sinful lives, the Apostle Paul reminds us:

*"What benefit had you then in those things*
*of which you are now ashamed?*

*For the end of those things is death."*

-Romans 6:21

And St. Augustine of Hippo reminds us that:

*"There is no saint without a past;*
*no sinner without a future."*

## John Newton and William Wilberforce

Whose life could give us more hope for a new start, than that of the former slave ship Captain, John Newton (1725-1807)?

He became a Christian Pastor (Anglican Priest), joining William Wilberforce (1759-1833), a Christian member of Parliament, fighting to outlaw the slave trade in the British Empire.

They accomplished this Herculean task after twenty years, in 1807, when England's Empire comprised one-fifth of the world.

## Amazing Grace

Wilberforce continued working to abolish slavery in the British Empire, and this was finally accomplished in 1833.

William Wilberforce went home to be with the Lord three days after legislation to abolish slavery passed Parliament.

Composing the words to the Hymn *Amazing Grace,* Newton stated it this way:

*"Though none go with me,*
*still I will follow."*

# 4.3  Mentors of Prayer

*"There is no wonder more supernatural and divine
in the life of a believer
than the mystery and ministry of prayer...*

*the hand of the child
touching the arm of the Father
and moving the wheel of the universe."*

-A.B. Simpson (1843-1919)
Founder: Christian & Missionary Alliance Church

**Seven Inspiring Saints of God**

T he lives of scores of godly men and women of prayer have had a deep influence on both Lay Monk Linda and myself in our ministry.

Of the multitude of Christian saints whose lives have influenced us in our prayer lives, we will now take a closer look at seven.

Four of them are in this chapter: *Martin Luther, Brother Lawrence, David Brainerd, and E.M. Bounds, and* three more are in Chapter 5: *Charles Spurgeon, Hudson Taylor, and George Müller.*

**A Martin Luther Prayer Tip:**

**To Be On God's Side, Follow God's Word and Your Conscience**

The man who began the Protestant Reformation while still an Augustinian monk, taught us that if we are on God's side, we are on the right side, no matter if the entire world unites against us.

Luther also taught us that to be on God's side, we need to follow the Word of God and our conscience.  We learned the truth of his words:

*"With God, one is a majority."*

**A Brother Lawrence Prayer Tip:**

**Live in Constant Awareness of God's Presence**

A Carmelite monk who remained a monk throughout his life, Brother Lawrence taught us to be aware of God's presence at all times, and that:

*"Our only business is to love
and delight ourselves in God."*

———

*"Think often on God, by day, by night,
in your business and even in your diversions.*

*He is always near you and with you;
leave Him not alone."*

**A David Brainerd Prayer Tip:**

**Pray to be a Witness for God and Make a Difference**

The buckskin-clad missionary to the native tribes of North America (1718-1747), wore himself out with extended prayer and mission work in the icy snowdrifts of the American wilderness.

Broken in health and dying of tuberculosis at the young age of 29, he taught us about being on fire for God: on fire for prayer, and on fire to preach the Gospel. Brainerd recorded his thoughts in his diary, only read by Jonathan Edwards (1703-1758) after Brainerd's death:

*"I care not where I go, or how I live,
or what I endure, so that I may save souls.*

*When I sleep, I dream of them;
when I awake, they are first in my thoughts."*

*"Lord, let me make a difference for you
that is utterly disproportionate
to who I am."*

**An E.M. Bounds Prayer Tip:**

**Begin Your Mornings With Prayer**

Rev. Bounds (1835-1913) inspires us with fervor to actually want to get down on our knees and pray, and to devote much more time to prayer than we have been.

Bounds wrote:

*"The men who have done
the most for God
in this world
have been early
on their knees.*

*He who fritters away the early morning,
its opportunities and freshness,
in other pursuits
than seeking God*

*will make poor headway seeking Him
the rest of the day.*

*If God is not first
in our thoughts and efforts
in the morning,*

*He will be in the last place
the remainder of the day."*

Bounds' *classic book Power Through Prayer* was originally published with the title, *Preacher and Prayer.*

It was written specifically to Preachers: Pastors, Evangelists, Missionaries, and those in other ministries.

If none of these categories apply to you, don't let that stop you from reading it...*everything in this inspiring book applies to all Christians.*

S.G. Preston

## A Kneeling Christian Prayer Tip:

## Prayer is Necessary for Spiritual Growth

The book *The Kneeling Christian*, published in 1924, approaches the same quality and intensity as those of E.M. Bounds. Its author, who wished to remain anonymous, wrote:

> *"It is not too much to say that*
> *all growth in the spiritual life –*
> *all victory over temptation,*
>
> *all confidence and peace*
> *in the presence of difficulties and dangers,*
>
> *all repose of spirit*
> *in times of great disappointment or loss,*
> *all habitual communion with God –*
>
> *depend upon the practice*
> *of secret prayer."*

Let's see what we can learn from the exemplary prayer lives of these great saints of God.

# 4.4  Martin Luther

*"Unless I am convicted by Scripture*
*and plain reason*

*(I do not accept the authority of popes and councils*
*because they have contradicted each other),*

*my conscience is captive to the Word of God.*

*I cannot and will not recant anything,*
*for to go against conscience*
*is neither right nor safe.*

*Here I stand, I can do no other.*
*So help me God.  Amen."*

-Martin Luther (1521)

**Luther In Hiding**

In January of 1521, Pope Leo X excommunicated Martin Luther. Luther was called upon to defend his beliefs three months later at the Church's Diet of Worms (Pronounced "Dee-it of Verms").

A Diet is an official assembly; Worms is the town in Germany where this one was held.  The Assembly was held before the Holy Roman Emperor Charles V.

This is where Luther made his famous refusal to recant.  The Emperor declared Luther a heretic and an outlaw.  Luther had refused to attend the Diet without a "safe conduct" agreement to come and go, and on his journey home he was kidnapped.

Though no one knew it at the time, it was a friendly "kidnapping" by Luther's supporter Frederick III (the Wise), Elector of Saxony.

**Translating the New Testament**

Luther grew a beard, and in addition adopted a clothing disguise and a fictitious name.

Frederick hid Luther in Wartburg Castle for a year, and Luther used the time to translate the New Testament into common vernacular German. His translation is still in use in Germany today.

Martin Luther refused for his entire lifetime to accept royalties for any of his numerous writings. In just one year, he had 133 works published. The Elector of Saxony provided Luther with a salary on which to live and support his wife and children. They made their home in Luther's former monastery, also given to him by the Elector.

## Half of Europe Sought His Death

How can enough ever be said of the German monk who singlehandedly began the Protestant Reformation? Oct. 31, 1517, Martin Luther nailed his *95 Theses* to the door of Wittenburg Cathedral. This day is celebrated in many Protestant Churches as *Reformation Day*. We here celebrate it every year.

Can we imagine what it would be like to have half of Europe, including its powerful religious establishments, and all the power of its many governments, seeking our death? No, I do not think that we can.

## Here I Stand

My favorite book on Martin Luther and the Reformation is: *"Here I Stand: A Life of Martin Luther"* by Roland Bainton. As far as films go, out of all the seemingly innumerable productions on Luther that we have viewed, two are *must see*:

*"Luther,"* starring Joseph Fiennes, a full-length feature film which was originally released in theatres, and:

*"PBS: Martin Luther,"* the excellent *"made for television"* docudrama, which explains and covers the various doctrinal divisions and issues, more thoroughly and in depth than the film *Luther*.

Although we have collected perhaps twenty films and videos about Martin Luther, we have preferred to watch the two mentioned above: many, many times each.

Most Protestants do not belong to any of the Lutheran Church communions, yet in some sense every Protestant is indeed a *Lutheran*.

What then, is to be learned from Martin Luther specifically concerning prayer?

**Luther's Prayer Life**

Of all the Protestant Reformers, perhaps none was more passionate than Luther, whose intensity infused every aspect of his life. I have quoted him elsewhere, that Martin Luther believed prayer to be as indispensable to the Christian life as breathing.

**A Martin Luther Prayer Tip:**

**Be Consistent in Prayer**

In Luther's prayer life, we also find a daily consistency of practice.

*"I judge that my prayer is
more than the Devil himself.*

*If it were otherwise,
Luther would have fared differently
long before this.*

*Yet men will not see and acknowledge
the great wonders or miracles
God works on my behalf.*

*If I should neglect prayer
but a single day,
I should lose a great deal
of the fire of faith."*

144

S.G. Preston

**A Martin Luther Prayer Tip:**

**Spend Much Time in Prayer**

Luther stressed that *much time* should be spent in prayer.  We will see this theme repeated often in the lives of many of the others whose lives of prayer inspire us.

> *"If I fail to spend two hours in prayer*
> *each morning,*
> *the Devil gets the victory*
> *throughout the day..."*

———

> *"...I have so much business,*
> *I cannot get on without spending*
> *three hours daily in prayer."*

**A Martin Luther Prayer Truth:**

**Praying Well Is Studying Well**

Martin Luther taught:

> *"He that has prayed well,*
> *has studied well."*

# 4.5  Brother Lawrence

*"Is giorra cabhair Dé ná an doras'."*
*"God's help is closer than the door."*

-Old Gaelic Saying

———

*"Each day presents a new opportunity*
*to experience God's presence."*

-A.W. Tozer
Christian & Missionary Alliance

## Practicing the Presence of God

Frenchman Nicholas Herman of Lorraine was born in 1611, and would live until 1691. He would become, first a Christian at the age of eighteen, and then a Carmelite monk known as Brother Lawrence.

Like Francis of Assisi, as a young man Nicholas was a soldier. After becoming a monk, he lived a quiet life performing various duties in the kitchen of his monastery. He taught:

> *"That we ought not to be weary*
> *of doing little things for the love of God,*
> *who regards not the greatness of the work,*
> *but the love with which it is performed."*

Brother Lawrence continually *practiced the presence of God* while working with his pots and pans. With his own life for our example, he shows a way for us to follow the Apostle Paul's teaching to *pray without ceasing,* while performing our daily routine required tasks.

In Paul's case, this sometimes included sewing tents.

**A Way of Prayer Observed in the Ancient Church**

When we look at Charles Spurgeon (1834-1892), we shall see that Spurgeon taught and practiced his own form of this; thereby endorsing the concept as one of *good sound Baptist teaching!*

I have already mentioned that John Chrysostom (c. 349-407 A.D.) taught this same truth:

> *"Of course, the prayer I have in mind*
> *is no matter of routine.*
>
> *It is deliberate and earnest…*
> *it is a state that endures night and day."*

**Maximus the Confessor**

This way of prayer was also taught by others in the Early Church, including Maximus the Confessor (580-662 A.D.).

*Confessor* was the designation given to one who had suffered much for the faith; often, like Maximus, undergoing extreme torture; but without being martyred.

Maximus wrote:

> *"Unceasing prayer*
> *means to*
> *have the mind*
> *always turned to God*
> *with great love;*
>
> *holding alive*
> *our hope in Him,*
> *having confidence*
> *in Him*
> *whatever we are doing,*
> *and whatever*
> *happens to us."*

## A Way to Experience Peace and Joy

When talking to individuals, Brother Lawrence shared with them his repeated efforts to keep his attention focused on God, no matter what business was occupying him.

He reports that this continual turning of his thoughts toward God eventually became effortless and filled him with peace and joy. In the book, *The Practice of the Presence of God*, we read:

*"The first time I saw Brother Lawrence*
*was upon the 3rd of August, 1666.*

*He told me that God*
*had done him a singular favor,*
*in his conversion at the age of eighteen...*

*...that he had been footman to M. Fieubert,*
*the treasurer,*
*and that he was a great awkward fellow*
*who broke everything.*

*That he had desired to be received into a monastery,*
*thinking...that he would there be made to smart*
*for his awkwardness and the faults he should commit,*
*and so he should sacrifice to God his life,*
*with its pleasures;*

*but that God had disappointed him,*
*he having met with nothing but satisfaction*
*in that state."*

Brother Lawrence taught:

*"...that in difficulties we need only*
*have recourse to Jesus Christ,*
*and beg His grace,*
*with which everything became easy."*

S.G. Preston

# 4.6  David Brainerd

*"Give yourself to prayer,*
*to reading and meditation on divine truths:*

*strive to penetrate to the bottom of them*
*and never be content with a superficial knowledge."*

*"Here am I, send me;*

*send me to the ends of the earth;*
*send me to the rough, the savage lost of the wilderness;*

*send me from all that is called comfort on earth;*
*send me even to death itself, if it be, but in Your service,*
*and to promote your kingdom."*

-David Brainerd (1718-1747)
Missionary to Native Americans

**Death at Age 29**

David Brainerd is someone whose life of prayer has had a tremendous effect on multitudes of Christians, from his own Colonial American Era and continuing through today.

At a time when there was still almost no interest in missions among Christians *throughout the entire world*, Brainerd felt a tremendous burden to fulfill Christ's Great Commission by reaching North American Indian tribes with the Gospel.

He took the Good News to the Delaware Indians of New Jersey, and also to Native Americans in New York State, Massachusetts, and Pennsylvania.

From his diary, we hold the poignant vision in our minds of David Brainerd trudging through deep snow to share the Gospel with the lost; praying for hours out of doors in snowdrifts, all the while coughing his lungs out in extreme sickness. He would soon die from tuberculosis.

## A Private Prayer Diary

David Brainerd went home to be with the Lord at the age of 29, while being cared for in the home of another profoundly inspirational Christian man of prayer: Jonathan Edwards.

After the young man's untimely death, Jonathan Edwards edited the book, *The Life and Diary of David Brainerd*, into the form in which we now have it.  Here are selections from the diary:

*"My soul felt a pleasing yet painful concern
lest I should spend some moments without God.*

*Oh, may I always live to God!*

*In the evening I was visited by some friends,
and spent the time in prayer,
and such conversation as tended to edification.*

*It was a comfortable season to my soul."*

———

*"I felt an ardent desire to spend every moment
with God.
God is unspeakably gracious to me continually.*

*In time past, He has given me
inexpressible sweetness in the performance of duty.*

*Frequently my soul has enjoyed much of God,
but has been ready to say,
'Lord, it is good to be here,'
and so indulge sloth while I have lived
on the sweetness of my feelings.*

*But of late God has been pleased
to keep my soul hungry almost continually,
so that I have been filled with a pleasing pain.*

*When I really enjoy God, I feel my desire of Him
more insatiable, and my thirsting after holiness
the more unquenchable."*

## One Solitary Life of Prayer

Brainerd's burden for the lost, deep godliness, and sweet spirit of prayer would profoundly affect Jonathan Edwards.

Edwards would later be the catalyst for Colonial America's Great Awakening revival, manifested through the preaching of George Whitefield and John Wesley.

> *"Cha'n 'eil gach iuchair 's an crochadh ria on chrios."*
>
> *"All the keys in the land do not hang from one belt."*
>
> -Old Gaelic Saying

## Making Films Recording Christian History

Excellent Christian Films have been made about the lives of almost all the great men of prayer I am about to mention.

It is amazing how often *one single life lived for Christ* inspires and influences other Christians, and actually *changes the history of the world.*

These Films are available through *Vision Video*, which offers over 2,000 Films. It was founded by Producer and movie-maker Ken Curtis (1939-2011), who was also responsible for making many of them.

## Ken Curtis

Besides *Vision Video*, Ken Curtis was the founder of *Gateway Films*, the *Christian History Institute* and *Christian History Magazine,* our favorite magazine.

I was blessed to be able to correspond with him briefly once, about Celtic Christian films, before he went home to be with the Lord in 2011.

His son Bill Curtis is now President of *Vision Video*, which has been of such help to us in our study of Christian History, and to our ministry, as well as to so many other Christians.

### *Timeline:* **John Wycliffe / Jan Hus / David Brainerd / The Great Awakening / The World Missions Movement**

> *"What are your choices?*
> *Whom are your choices for?*
> *Not just for yourself.*
>
> *Choose now whom you will serve,*
> *and that choice is going to affect*
> *the next generation,*
> *and the next generation,*
> *and the next.*
>
> *Choice never affects just one person alone.*
>
> *It goes on and on*
> *and the effect goes out*
> *into geography and history.*
>
> *You are part of history*
> *and your choices*
> *become part of history."*

-Edith Schaeffer (1914-2013) Author: *"L'Abri"*

What do the lives of John Wycliffe and Jan Hus have to do with the Great Awakening revival in America, nearly three-hundred years after their deaths? And even later, with the World Missions Movement of the 1800's?

Quite a bit, it turns out:

**1384: John Wycliffe's (1330-1384) translation of the New Testament from Latin into English is completed.**

S.G. Preston

His students would finish John's translation of the Old Testament after his death. Wycliffe is known as *"The Morning Star of the Reformation."*

From Wycliffe's reading and study of Holy Scripture, he came to the same doctrinal conclusions that the later Protestant Reformers would later arrive at independently.

Among these: that the Bible is the sole and final authority for Christian Life and Doctrine, and the rejection of the claim of the Papacy to authority over all Christians. Wycliffe called upon the English government to reform the Church.

## The Lollards

He also founded an Order of Lay preachers called the *Lollards* to spread the Gospel throughout England. They are generally recognized as a precursor movement to the Protestant Reformation. We also consider them to be an early pre-cursor of the New Monasticism and Lay Monasticism movements.

John Wycliffe was so beloved by both the people of England and internationally, that the Church authorities feared to excommunicate him during his lifetime.

Instead, they waited until thirty years after his death. Wycliffe's teachings were then condemned at the Council of Constance. They ordered his bones to be dug up and burnt (because they were unable to burn him at the stake during his lifetime). Then they dumped his ashes in a river. This last was symbolical of drowning him.

## Foxe's Book of Martyrs

John Foxe wrote about John Wycliffe:

> *"...though they dug up his body,*
> *burnt his bones, and drowned his ashes,*
> *yet the Word of God*
> *and the truth of his doctrine,*

153

*with the fruit and success thereof,*
*they could not burn;*
*which yet to this day...doth remain."*

*Wycliffe Bible Translators* is named in honor of him. John Wycliffe's English translation Bibles still had to be copied individually by hand; William Tyndale's later translation of the Bible would become the first *printed* version in English.

**1415: Jan Hus (or: John Huss, 1370-1415) is burned at the stake by Church authorities for spreading the teachings of John Wycliffe.** Teachings that 100 years later, when Martin Luther taught the same, would be called Protestant Doctrines.

The martyrdom of Hus sparked the Moravian revival in Bohemia. Hus means *goose.* Luther considered Hus' prediction, given immediately before Hus was burned at the stake, to be about Luther himself:

*"They might now be*
*roasting a goose,*
*but in a hundred years*
*they will hear a swan sing,*
*which they will*
*not be able to silence."*

**1517: Martin Luther, an Augustinian monk, begins the Protestant Reformation by nailing his 95 Theses to the door of Wittenburg Cathedral.** He translates the Bible from Latin into the German language.

**1535: William Tyndale's (c. 1494-1536) translation of the Bible into English was completed by Miles Coverdale and printed.** Tyndale was greatly influenced by both John Wycliffe and Martin Luther.

William was forced to go into hiding on the Continent. His translation of the New Testament had to be printed there, and then smuggled into England. All copies were burned by the authorities when discovered.

**Punishable by Death**

For the crime of translating the New Testament into English, agents from England (it is not known whether the actual order was given by Henry VIII, Thomas More, or Bishop Stokely of London) hunted Tyndale down, convicted him of heresy, and executed him by strangling, immediately before burning him at the stake. His last words were a prayer:

*"Lord, open the King of England's eyes."*

His prayer was answered only two years later, when Henry VIII authorized publication of the *Great Bible*, an English translation.

**1611: The *King James Version* of the Bible is published.** It is believed to be heavily based on Tyndale's translation: as much as 83% of the New Testament, and 76% of the Old Testament.

**1706: August Francke (1663-1727) founds a Christian Orphanage and *"prays in"* the funds for it without soliciting them or asking anyone for money except God.** He pioneered in modern times what we now call: *"living on faith."* Both the orphanage and the practice of funding it through *prayer alone* inspires George Müller to do the same in the 1890's.

Francke Founds a Bible School, and sends two of its students as missionaries to India.

**1722: Count Zinzendorf (1700-1760), a Lutheran *Pietist* (similar in belief to today's Evangelicals), allows Moravians fleeing persecution to live on his land.**

The Moravians for the past 300 years have been followers of Jan Hus, who was influenced by the teachings of John Wycliffe.

**Sometime in 1732, Zinzendorf sends two Moravian missionaries: Johann Leonhard Dober and David Nitschman, to bring the Gospel to the slaves on the Caribbean Island of St. Thomas in the Caribbean.**

Count Zinzendorf and the Moravians were early opponents of slavery. The Quakers (Society of Friends) also began opposing slavery in the 1750's, and were an inspiration to William Wilberforce (Note: the first person in the ancient world to oppose slavery (in the 400's A.D.). was also a Christian: St. Patrick.

**1738: Moravian Missionaries convert Charles and John Wesley to Christ.**

**1730's-70's: Jonathan Edwards, along with George Whitefield, and John Wesley, all three great men of prayer, ignite America's Great Awakening revival.** They teach and popularize an *Evangelical* Theology of the need for individual, personal salvation: a conversion experience.

This had already been, for 200 years, the Evangelical teaching of the Lutheran Pietist movement, begun in the 1500's, of which Count Zinzendorf, 200 years later in the 1700's, was a member.

**1747: David Brainerd, a man of great prayer; and a missionary to the Native Americans in the states of Massachusetts, New York, New Jersey, and Pennsylvania, succumbs to death from Tuberculosis at the very young age of 29.** Jonathan Edwards reads and publishes Brainerd's prayer-saturated Diary.

**1793: Englishman William Carey is inspired by reading David Brainerd's Diary to travel to India as a missionary.**

**1956: Jim Elliot (1927-1956), like Jonathan Edwards and William Carey, is greatly inspired by David Brainerd's Diary.** Like Brainerd, Elliott died at age 29, one of five missionaries martyred in Ecuador while attempting to bring the Gospel to the native Huaorani people during *"Operation Auca"* (like Lay Monk Linda, he is from Portland, Oregon).

## William Carey and David Brainerd

*Carey's Brotherhood,* consisting of a deeply dedicated group of missionaries in Serampore, India, had this to say about David Brainerd:

> *"Let us look often at Brainerd*
> *in the woods of America*
> *pouring out his very soul before God*
> *for the perishing heathen*
> *without whose salvation*
> *nothing could make him happy.*
>
> *Prayer -- secret fervent believing prayer --*
> *lies at the root of all personal godliness.*
>
> *A competent knowledge of the language*
> *where a missionary lives,*
> *a mild and winning temper,*
> *a heart given up to God*
> *in private prayer room religion –*
>
> *these, these are the attainments which,*
> *more than all knowledge, or all other gifts,*
> *will fit us to become*
> *the instruments of human redemption."*

## R.A. Torrey and Dr. J. Vernon McGee

R.A. Torrey (1856-1928) was appointed the first President of the Moody Bible Institute.

He succeeded Dwight Moody (1837-1899) in his worldwide ministry of evangelism, when Moody died unexpectedly during an evangelistic tour.

Torrey later founded *The Church of the Open Door* in Los Angeles, California, and upon his own death, was in turn succeeded in that pulpit by Dr. J. Vernon McGee (1904-1988). Our own Lay Monk Bob (1926-2015) once visited this Church while Dr. McGee was its Pastor.

## Thru the Bible

After his retirement as a Church Pastor, Dr. McGee began teaching a once-a-week, half-hour Bible program on a local Pasadena, California radio station. He proved to be a popular and gifted radio Bible teacher; teaching the entire Bible through every five years.

Dr. McGee is also the author of over 100 Christian books, explaining and teaching the message of the Bible. He founded the *Thru the Bible* worldwide radio ministry, which continues expanding exponentially into hundreds of countries and languages, decades after he went home to be with the Lord. We have been blessed by his teaching for many years.

Dr. McGee, speaking of his very first visiting preaching assignment, said:

*"After a morning service, he came to speak to me.*
*He groped for words, then blurted out,*
*'I never knew Jesus was so wonderful!'*

*He started to say more but choked up*
*and hurried out of the church.*

*As I watched him stride across the field, I prayed,*
*'Oh God, help me to always preach*
*so that it can be said,*

*'I never knew Jesus was so wonderful.'"*

158

S.G. Preston

### R.A. Torrey: "And God heard David Brainerd..."

In the following quote, R.A. Torrey uses the old term *consumption* for what we now call tuberculosis. Torrey wrote this about David Brainerd (Boldface mine, for emphasis):

> *"The mighty men of God,*
> *who throughout the centuries*
> *have wrought great things by prayer,*
> *are the men who have had*
> *much painful toil in prayer.*
>
> *Take for example, David Brainerd,*
> *that physically feeble,*
> *but spiritually mighty man of God.*
>
> *Trembling for years on the verge of consumption,*
> *from which he ultimately died at an early age,*
>
> *Brainerd felt led of God to labor among*
> *the North American Indians in the early days,*
> *in the primeval forests of northern Pennsylvania;*
>
> *and sometimes of a winter night*
> *he would go out into the forest,*
> *and kneel in the cold snow when it was a foot deep,*
> *and so labor with God in prayer*
> *that he would be wringing wet with perspiration;*
> *even out in the cold winter night hours.*
>
> ***And God heard David Brainerd,***
> *and sent such a mighty revival*
> *among the North American Indians*
> *as had never been heard of before;*
> *as indeed had never been dreamed about."*

159

# 4.7 E.M. Bounds

(Boldface mine.)
*"This unction* (anointing) *is not the gift of genius.*
*It is not found in the halls of learning.*

*No eloquence can woo it. No industry can win it.*
*No prelatical hands can confer it.*

*It is the gift of God – the signet set to his own messengers.*

*It is **heaven's knighthood***

*given to the chosen true and brave ones*
*who have sought this anointed honor*
*through many an hour of tearful,*
*wrestling prayer."*

-E.M. Bounds (1835-1913)

### Pastor in Missouri During the Civil War

Edward McKendree Bounds, though a civilian Methodist Pastor, was arrested for opposing the confiscation of his church building by the Union Army. He was placed in a Union prison, serving during his captivity as a Chaplain to Confederate prisoners.

After the war, and his eventual retirement as a Pastor, he began writing books on prayer. It is said that he prayed daily from four to seven every morning before beginning work on his writings.

As to the importance and effect of prayer on the believer, Rev. Bounds wrote:

*"Walking with God down the avenue of prayer*
*we acquire something of His likeness,*
*and unconsciously we become witnesses to others*
*of His beauty and His grace."*

S.G. Preston

## Motivating Us to Pray

Apart from the Holy Scriptures themselves, we consider E.M. Bounds' books to be the most motivating writings regarding prayer ever to be put down on paper, though others might contend that David Brainerd's Diary holds this place.

For Pastor Bounds, any lack in the Church rests with the individual Christian. *We* are the problem, but by God's grace, we can also be a part of the solution; *if* we consecrate ourselves to God and give ourselves to prayer.

## The Holy Spirit Anoints Men and Women of Prayer

In his classic book, *Power Through Prayer*, E.M. Bounds contrasted the use of various *"novel methods"* in the church with the need for more Christians mighty in prayer:

> *"What the Church needs to-day*
> *is not more machinery, or better,*
> *not new organizations*
> *or more and novel methods,*
> *but men whom the Holy Ghost can use –*
> *men of prayer, men mighty in prayer.*
>
> *The Holy Ghost does not flow through methods,*
> *but through men.*
> *He does not come on machinery, but on men.*
> *He does not anoint plans, but men –*
> *men of prayer."*

## An E.M. Bounds Prayer Tip:

## Pray With Your Entire Being

For E.M. Bounds, prayer is an integral part of our life in Christ. Bounds believed prayer is the solution to all that ails us, and to all that ails the Church:

*"Our whole being must be in our praying;*
*like John Knox, we must say and feel,*
*'Give me Scotland or I die.'*

*Our experience and revelations of God are born*
*of our costly sacrifice, of our costly conflicts,*
*our costly praying.*

*The wrestling and all night praying of Jacob*
*made an era never to be forgotten in Jacob's life,*
*brought God to the rescue,*
*changed Esau's attitude and conduct,*
*changed Jacob's character, saved and affected his life*
*and entered into the habits of a nation."*

## John Fletcher

As expressed in the Bible, E.M. Bounds agreed that the lives of holy men and women of God throughout history are given to us as examples to emulate. He wrote about John Fletcher (1729-1785):

*"John Fletcher stained the walls of his room*
*by the breath of his prayers.*

*Sometimes he would pray all night;*
*always, frequently, and with great earnestness.*
*His whole life was a life of prayer.*

*'I would not rise from my seat,' he said,*
*'without lifting my heart to God.'*
*His greeting to a friend was always:*
*'Do I meet you praying?"*

## The Necessity of Being Much Alone With God

John Fletcher was the hand-picked successor of the great Evangelist John Wesley (1703-1791), the Anglican Priest who Founded the Methodist movement. Fletcher was quoted earlier in the first chapter of this book.

162

Although John Fletcher had indeed been a great man of prayer throughout his Christian life, yet on his deathbed he still sorrowed that he had not spent *even more* of the previous fifty years of his life in prayer.

E.M. Bounds believed that any Christian of true faith *will* want to spend much time with God in prayer. But that it needs to be quality time:

> *"We would not have any think*
> *that the value of their prayers*
> *is to be measured by the clock,*
>
> *but our purpose*
> *is to impress on our minds*
> *the necessity of being*
> *much alone with God;*
> *and that if this feature has not been*
> *produced by our faith,*
> *then our faith is of a feeble*
> *and surface type."*

## The Prayer Lifestyle of E.M. Bounds

The writings of E. M. Bounds are a motivator to grow in prayer, because he actually *lived* a life of prayer.

Lyle W. Dorsett's book, *E.M. Bounds: Man of Prayer*, tells the story of how Rev. Bounds felt called to take a train to attend a Christian event, and decided that it would be good to take one of his young sons with him.

The only problem was that Bounds didn't have enough money for the tickets.

He talked to the Conductor, telling the train official how much money he had, and asking him to let them ride as far as their money allowed, and then to put them off the train at that point.

## God Had Called Them

E.M Bounds had confidence God would get them where God had called them to go. The Conductor looked at the money and was shocked. He exclaimed, "But I'll be putting you off in a farmer's field in the middle of nowhere!"

Just then a man blessed by Bound's ministry walked up to them, and said he would be honored to pay for the tickets for Rev. Bounds and his son.

## An E.M. Bounds Prayer Tip

### Spending Much Time With God is the Secret of Successful Prayer

Yes, E.M. Bounds really was a dedicated, holy man of God: a man of prayer. How wonderful it would be if we could all say this of ourselves! He has given us many examples of great lives of prayer in his writings.

Charles Simeon was a great man of prayer, a Calvinist Pastor who, with the Calvinist Evangelist, George Whitefield, was friends with a third great man of prayer, the Arminian John Wesley:

*"The men who have most fully illustrated Christ*
*in their character, and have most powerfully affected*
*the world for Him, have been men who spent so much time*
*with God as to make it a notable feature of their lives.*

*Charles Simeon devoted the hours*
*from four till eight in the morning to God.*
*Mr. Wesley spent two hours daily in prayer.*
*He began at four in the morning.*

*Of him, one who knew him well wrote: 'He thought*
*prayer to be more his business than anything else,*
*and I have seen him leave his prayer room*
*with a serenity of face next to shining.'"*

164

S.G. Preston

**An E.M. Bounds Prayer Tip**

**The Effectiveness of Short Prayers is Dependent On...**

Pastor Bounds wrote eleven books during his lifetime. Nine are about prayer, and only about prayer. Each chapter is devoted to a different aspect of prayer.

Bounds speaks of the practices of great men of prayer; and of spending *much time* in prayer, that we might have *much power* in our prayers:

*"While many private prayers,*
*in the nature of things, must be short;*
*while public prayers, as a rule,*
*ought to be short and condensed;*

*while there is ample room for and value*
*put on spontaneous vocal prayer—*

*yet in our private communions with God,*
*time is a feature essential to its value.*

*Much time spent with God*
*is the secret of all successful praying.*

*Prayer which is felt as a mighty force*
*is the mediate or immediate product*
*of much time spent with God.*

*Our short prayers owe their point and efficiency*
*to the long ones that have preceded them.*

*The short prevailing prayer cannot be prayed*
*by one who has not prevailed with God*
*in a mightier struggle of long continuance."*

\* \* \*

# *Answers to Prayer*
## *PrayerFoundation 24-Hr. Prayerchain*

### Nov. 27, 2001 - Answer to Prayer

My Aunt Esther has liver, bone, and brain Cancer. They have not found the source. She did not have the Chemotherapy, like my Mom, and now is doing so much better. Aunt Esther's cancer was spreading rapidly, even more than my Mom's.

Thank you, so much for all your prayers. She has had a turnaround and is improving. Please continue to pray for Aunt Esther. She is very thin, under 100 pounds.

She is home, and is improving, very much. Praise The Lord!

Please pray they find the source of the Cancer. God Bless You! God Bless the *PrayerFoundation*, and all the *Prayer Warriors*, and Monks.

Thank you so much for all your prayers.

### (Also) Nov. 27, 2001 - Urgent Prayer Request:

Please continue to pray for Aunt Esther and my Mom, Helena. Please pray for a miracle in both these sweet ladies. Please pray for God's will for my Mom; for her terminal Cancer.

The Doctor has been saying that she has days. She is bleeding internally from the chemotherapy. Her body is shutting down. She has liver and bone Cancer.

### Answer to Prayer - Nov. 28, 2001 (One day later.)

Thank you so very much for all your prayers. My Mom, Helena, has had a turn around and is drinking and eating for the first time in six weeks.

Praise The Lord! Thank You, Jesus! Thank You All! I so deeply appreciate everyone at the *PrayerFoundation* for all your support

S.G. Preston

and prayers. It is truly a miracle from *God!* Thank You Jesus, and all the *Prayer Warriors*, and the Monks. Thank You Jesus, for this Miracle. It is purely miraculous.

The Doctor was giving my Mom a day to live (yesterday). The family was making funeral arrangements.

This Tuesday morning, my Mom was talking and ravenously hungry. She ate today more than she ate in 6 weeks all together.

Praise Jesus, for He does answer prayers. Amen! Thank You, God for all of the Blessings! Thank You, God, for all the Miracles! God Bless Everyone!

### Answer to Prayer - Update Dec. 6, 2001 (Eight Days Later)

My Mom has had a *Miracle!* She has been healed from Cancer, and now is being healed from Chemotherapy.

Praise The Lord! Thank You, *Jesus!* On Saturday, my Mom is being released from Hospice! Praise God! It is a miracle, since last week the Doctor said she would not last a day. The family had started to make funeral arrangements.

Praise The Lord! It is a *Miracle!!!! Jesus Still Heals!!!!!!!!!!!* It is eight days since the Doctor said that. Praise *God!!!!!!!!!!!!!*

---

(From the book: *Answers to Prayer* by S.G. Preston)

167

## Thought, Word, and Deed:

*"For though we walk in the flesh, we do not war after the flesh:
for the weapons of our warfare are not carnal,
but mighty through God to the pulling down of strongholds;
casting down imaginations, and every high thing
that exalts itself against the knowledge of God,
and bringing into captivity every thought
to the obedience of Christ."*

-2nd Corinthians 10:3-5

*"Finally, brethren, whatever things are true, whatever things are
honest, whatever things are just, whatever things are pure,
whatever things are lovely, whatever things are of good report; If
there is any virtue, and if there is any praise; think on these things.*

*Those things, which you have both learned, and received,
and heard, and seen in me, do:
and the God of peace shall be with you."*

-Philippians 4:8-9

*"And whatever you do in word or deed,
do all in the name of the Lord Jesus,
giving thanks to God the Father through Him."*

-Colossians 3:17

*"But the fruit of the Spirit is love, joy, peace,
Patience, gentleness, goodness
faithfulness, humility, self-control."*

*"Since we live in the Spirit, let us also walk in the Spirit."*

-Galatians 5:22-23,25

\* \* \*

# 5: *Spurgeon, Taylor, Müller*

## 5.1 Great Prayer Christians

*"Of course, the preacher is above all others*
*distinguished as a man of prayer.*
*He prays as an ordinary Christian, else he were a hypocrite.*

*He prays more than ordinary Christians,*
*else he were disqualified for the office he has undertaken.*

*If you, as ministers are not very prayerful,*
*you are to be pitied.*

*If you become lax in sacred devotion,*
*not only will you need to be pitied, but your people also,*

*and the day comes in which*
*you shall be ashamed and confounded.*

*All our libraries and studies are mere emptiness*
*compared with our prayer rooms.*

*Our seasons of fasting and prayer*
*at the Tabernacle have been high days indeed;*
*never has heaven's gate stood wider;*
*never have our hearts*
*been nearer the central Glory."*

-Charles Spurgeon (1834-1892) English Baptist
Pastor, *"The Prince of Preachers"*

### Hudson Taylor: Founding a Faith Ministry and Living On Faith

Charles Spurgeon, in agreement with Brother Lawrence, taught us to lift our thoughts in prayer to God continually throughout the day.

169

Spurgeon also encouraged us to go to the Word of God in prayer, to more clearly hear what God would say to us.

Hudson Taylor founded the *China Inland Mission*, the first missionary organization to send missionaries into the vast interior of China, ultimately comprising half of all the total missionaries sent to that empire.

Hudson taught us about humility, and having a burning passion to fulfill Christ's Great Commission. In common with George Müller and with Francis and Edith Schaeffer, Hudson taught us about *living on faith*, and operating our entire ministry on the same principle.

> *"God wants you to have something*
> *far better than riches and gold,*
> *and that is helpless dependence upon Him."*

> ———

> *"I have found that there are three stages*
> *in every great work of God:*
> *First, it is impossible, then it is difficult,*
> *then it is done."*

## Inspired by *L'Abri* and St. Francis

It has already been said how the inspiration to found our ministry came from a trip to Ireland and Assisi, Italy. We were greatly inspired by the lives of the ancient Celtic monks, and the life of St. Francis.

The inspiration of how to organize and practice our ministry, came from an additional two sources.

The first example was Edith Schaeffer's amazing book, *L'Abri*, about her and her husband Francis Schaeffer's years of ministry in French Switzerland

The second was the portrayal of the early ministry of St. Francis in Franco Zefirelli's magnificent film: *Brother Sun, Sister Moon.*

It is our favorite film of all time, although Zefirelli is better known for his Film, *Romeo and Juliet*; and for the mini-series, *Jesus of Nazareth*.

## Faith Ministries

The life and ministries of August Francke, George Müller, Hudson Taylor, Francis Schaeffer (1912-1984) and Edith Schaeffer (1914-2013); inspired our own decision to *found a faith ministry*.

> *"And this is the confidence that we have in him,*
> *that if we ask anything according to his will,*
> *He hears us:*
>
> *and if we know that He hears us, whatever we ask,*
> *we know that we have the petitions*
> *that we desired of Him."*

> -1 John 5:14-15

These great practitioners of prayer taught us that we should expect an answer to every single prayer we pray, if it is grounded in the Word of God.

# 5.2  Charles Spurgeon

*"Make the most of prayer...
Prayer is the master weapon.*

*We should be wise if we used it more,
and did so with a
more specific purpose."*

-Charles Spurgeon (1834-1892) English Baptist Pastor, *"The
Prince of Preachers"*

## Over 6,000 Members

One hundred years ago, long before the megachurches of
today, Charles Spurgeon pastored a congregation consisting
of more than 6,000 members.

At the age of 20, in 1854, he had become pastor of *New Park
Street Chapel* (later: *Metropolitan Tabernacle*) in London, a
Reformed Baptist Church, when it had only 232 members.

## The Prince of Preachers

Many of the great theologians and preachers of the last century
have said that Spurgeon greatly influenced their spiritual lives.
These include such men as:

*J.C. Ryle,
George Müller, Hudson Taylor,
and Dwight Moody.*

Spurgeon is known as "The Prince of Preachers."  This was the
title given to him while he was still alive.

Charles Spurgeon was the John Chrysostom of his era.
*Chrysostom* means: *"Golden Mouth."*

This was the title given to John after his death.

## More Writings By Spurgeon Than By Any Other Christian

Augustine of Hippo and John Chrysostom of Constantinople had something in common: both were monks called against their will to pastor congregations.

These men were two of the most prolific writers and preachers of all eras, yet Spurgeon outdid them both.

We have more writings by Charles Spurgeon than by any other Christian in history. Spurgeon was famous for his sermons, but he was also a great man of prayer.

He was not a man of long seasons of prayer, but a man who, like Brother Lawrence, *practiced the presence of God.*

## Living a Prayer Lifestyle

It is said of Charles Spurgeon that he never prayed for more than five minutes at a time, and that he never went for more than five minutes without praying.

Often, he would take people on a tour of the *Metropolitan Tabernacle.* Reaching the basement Prayer Room where people were in constant prayer, Spurgeon would say:

*"Here is the powerhouse of this church."*

## A Godly Man of Prayer

His wife, who would certainly have known him best, said of him:

*"At the tea table, the conversation was bright,*
*witty, and always interesting;*

*and after the meal was over,*
*an adjournment was made to the study*
*for family worship,*

*and it was at these seasons*
*that my beloved's prayers*

*were remarkable for their tender childlikeness,*
*their spiritual pathos, and their intense devotion.*

*He seemed to come as near to God*
*as a little child to a loving father,*

*and we were often moved to tears*
*as he talked thus face to face*
*with his Lord."*

## Differing Strengths and Practices

There are many great men and women of prayer who have remained unknown while interceding for others.

But many of the most well-known of the leading missionaries and evangelists of their day were also great men and women of prayer.

They could not have lived the lives they lived, or seen the movements of God that they saw, had they been otherwise. Yet all had differing strengths and practices of prayer, and by looking at their lives, we may learn much from each of them.

## A Charles Spurgeon Prayer Tip:

## The Necessity of Intensity in Prayer

Charles Spurgeon taught that when we pray, we should pray with great intensity:

*"Prayer pulls the rope down below*
*and the great bell rings above in the ears of God.*

*Some scarcely stir the bell,*
*for they pray so languidly;*
*others give only an occasional jerk at the rope.*

*But he who communicates with heaven is the man who grasps the*
*rope boldly and pulls continuously*
*with all his might."*

S.G. Preston

## A John Climacus Prayer Tip:

## Intensity in Prayer is Faith

Among the Church Fathers, we find this view of prayer also expressed by John Climacus (d. 649 A.D.), author of *The Ladder of Divine Ascent*, a book written to help monks overcome temptation and grow in Christ. For John Climacus, this intensity in prayer that Spurgeon spoke of is nothing less than faith:

> *"Let all multiplicity (of words)*
> *be absent from your prayer.*
>
> *A single word was enough for the publican*
> *and the prodigal son to receive God's pardon...*
>
> *Do not try to find exactly*
> *the right words for your prayer:*
>
> *how many times does the simple*
> *and monotonous stuttering of children*
> *draw the attention of their father!*
>
> *Do not launch into long discourses,*
> *for if you do,*
> *your mind will be dissipated trying to find*
> *just the right words.*
>
> *The publican's short sentence*
> *moved God to mercy.*
> *A single word full of faith saved the thief."*

## A Charles Spurgeon Prayer Tip:

## Pray to Receive the Power of the Word of God

Charles Spurgeon taught:

> *"How are we to handle this sword of 'It is written'?*
> *First, with deepest reverence.*

*Let every word that God has spoken*
*be Law and Gospel to you.*

*Never trifle with it;*
*never try to evade its force*
*or change its meaning.*

*God speaks to you in this book*
*as much as if He came to the top of Sinai*
*and lifted up his voice with thunder.*

*I like to open the Bible and pray,*
*'Lord God, let the Word*
*leap off my page into my soul;*
*make it vivid, powerful,*
*and fresh to my heart.'*

*Our Lord Himself felt the power of the Word.*
*It was not so much the Devil who felt the power of*
*'It is written' as Christ Himself.*
*The manhood of Christ felt an awe*
*of the Word of God,*
*and so the Word*
*became a power to Christ.*

*To trifle with Scripture*
*is to deprive yourself of its aid.*

*Reverence it, and look up to God*
*with devout gratitude*
*for having given it to you."*

## A Charles Spurgeon Prayer Tip:

## Pray Until You Can Pray

How important was prayer to Charles Spurgeon?  How important did he think it was for the average Christian?

He has the following advice for all of us; I have to confess that it is one of my many all-time favorite quotes about prayer:

176

S.G. Preston

*"Pray until you can pray;*
*pray to be helped to pray*
*and do not give up praying*
*because you cannot pray.*

*For it is when you think you cannot pray;*
*that is when you are praying."*

# 5.3  Hudson Taylor

*"God always gives His very best
to those who leave the choice with Him."*

-Hudson Taylor (1832-1905)
Founder, *China Inland Mission*

### Go for Me to China

Although today's Chinese Christians are mostly unaware of him, the Christianity that exists in China today is due largely to the efforts of this *one* faithful man of prayer.  Before his birth, Hudson Taylor's godly parents prayed that if they had a son, he would become a missionary to China.

God eventually mightily answered their prayer, but it seemed for many years that He would not.  Hudson was very sickly as a child -- and he was not a Christian!

His parents gave up any hope that he would ever become a missionary.

### Hudson Gives His Life to Christ

When he turned seventeen, however, Hudson received Christ as his Lord and Savior.  He made a promise to God that he would go anywhere, do anything, and suffer anything for Christ.  One day he felt that he heard a distinct call from God:

*"Then go for Me to China."*

### Prayer and Living On Faith

Still in England, Hudson determined to *"live on faith."*  He entered Medical School as a preparation for his missionary work. Hudson denied himself many comforts and lived in extreme poverty, so as to be able to pay for his schooling.

He refused any offers of financial support. At one point, he nearly died from an extreme fever he contracted while attending school.

## Hudson Taylor and George Müller

In 1853, at the age of twenty-one, Hudson Taylor went to China as a missionary. However, the missionary society that sent him wasn't very well organized, and they often failed to send him money.

Hudson found he had no money to pay for food and rent. He prayed, and a donation arrived...from George Müller!

## Prayer and Giving

Müller not only *"prayed in"* all of the support for his own extensive orphanage and schooling ministries, he also continually gave away the equivalent of millions of dollars in today's money to hundreds of missionaries all over the world.

Yet Müller never solicited funds, or even made his needs known outside of his own ministry.

## Hudson Inspired by Müller

Following the example of George Müller, Hudson Taylor resigned from his Mission Board, trusting God to supply all his needs, and determined not to ask anyone other than God for money.

Hudson founded the *China Inland Mission* (CIM; later known as: *Overseas Missionary Fellowship,* and OMF *International*) on the same principles. All of the missionaries that he recruited were also required to *"live on faith."*

## God Will Provide

The missionaries of the *China Inland Mission* would have no guaranteed salaries, nor were they allowed to appeal for funds.

Hudson required them to simply trust God for supplying any needs. Hudson Taylor said:

*"Depend upon it. God's work, done in God's way,
will never lack for supplies."*

## Evangelizing China

Until Hudson arrived in China, there were only a very small number of missionaries in just a few of the coastal ports of China.

At the time of his death, after spending 51 years of his life in China, the CIM included 205 Mission stations with over 800 missionaries, and 125,000 Chinese Christians in eighteen provinces. It would become the largest missionary organization in the world.

## Recommended Book and Film

The story of his life is one of the most amazing and inspiring stories that we have ever heard. To learn about his life is to receive many spiritual blessings: *Hudson Taylor's Spiritual Secret* by Dr. Howard Taylor is our favorite book about this great man of prayer. Dr. Taylor is Hudson's son.

There is also a greatly inspiring Film on Hudson's life simply called: *Hudson Taylor* which we have watched many times. We have even played it for a group of young people from a visiting Christian missionary ministry.

## 1900 - The Boxer Rebellion

Hudson's message was:

*"China is not to be won for Christ by quiet,
ease-loving men and women...*

*The stamp of men and women we need
is such as will put Jesus,*
(and) *China souls*

180

S.G. Preston

> *first and foremost in everything*
> *and at every time –*
>
> *even life itself must be secondary."*

By the time of the Boxer Rebellion, an anti-foreigner reign of terror in 1900, half of all the missionaries in China were members of his organization.

During this horrific Rebellion, *most missionaries* and *over 2,000 Chinese Christians* were murdered, becoming martyrs for Christ.

# 5.4 George Müller

*"I live in the spirit of prayer;
I pray as I walk, when I lie down and when I rise,
and the answers are always coming."*

-George Müller (1805-1898)
Founder, Christian Orphanages and Schools
Founder, *Open Brethren Movement*
World Evangelist from Age 70 to Age 86

## 129 Million Dollars

**M**any of the greatest men and women of prayer were inspired by Müller's walk with God. These include: *Charles Spurgeon, Hudson Taylor, R.A. Torrey, Francis and Edith Schaeffer.*

Current terms such as *"faith ministry," "living on faith," "living on prayer,"* and other similar descriptive phrases can in many ways be best illustrated by looking at the way in which George Müller lived.

## August Francke

After learning about the life of August Francke (1663-1727), a Lutheran Pastor who founded Christian orphanages by *"praying in"* the funds for them.

Müller made the decision to found and operate his many ministries *without ever asking anyone other than God for finances*, exactly as Francke had done.

This included hundreds of schools: educating 120,000 children, and orphanages supporting 10,024 of children. His orphanages are still in existence today.

S.G. Preston

During his lifetime he *"prayed in,"* and gave away, the equivalent of 129 million dollars in today's money: U.S. Dollars in 2018, Gold valued at $1,300 an ounce.

## Stewardship of Money

Andrew Murray (1828-1917) wrote this about George Müller's view of money:

*"This implicit surrender to God's Word led him to certain views and conduct in regard to money, which mightily influenced his future life.*

*They had their root in the conviction that money was a Divine stewardship,*

*and that all money had therefore to be received and dispensed in direct fellowship with God Himself."*

## An Andrew Murray Prayer Truth:

## Definite Answer to Prayer is the Rule of Life

Andrew Murray wrote concerning this:

*"It is one of the terrible marks of the diseased state of Christian life in these days, that there are so many who rest content without the distinct experience of answer to prayer.*

*They pray daily, they ask many things, and trust that some of them will be heard,*

*but know little of direct definite answer to prayer as the rule of life.*

*And it is this the Father wills:*

*He seeks daily communication with His children in listening to and gaining their petitions."*

**A George Müller Prayer Tip:**

**Faith (Including for Prayer) Comes By Hearing the Word of God**

Andrew Murray also wrote about George Müller's view of God's Word:

> *"We find in his journal frequent mention made*
> *of his spending two and three hours*
> *in prayer over the Word*
> *for the feeding of his spiritual life.*
>
> *As the fruit of this, when he had need*
> *of strength and encouragement in prayer,*
>
> *the individual promises were not to him*
> *so many arguments from a book*
> *to be used with God,*
>
> *but living words which he had heard*
> *the Father's living voice speak to him,*
>
> *and which he could now bring to the Father*
> *in living faith."*

**A George Müller Prayer Tip:**

**Keep a Prayer Journal and Expect Your Prayers to Be Answered**

George Müller's Prayer Journal included what was basically a set of ledger books.

The date and prayer request were written in the column on the left, and the date and the answer to the prayer was written in the column on the right, when the prayer was answered.

Once George Müller had recorded a prayer request in his Prayer Journal, he would not cease praying for that prayer request until the prayer had been answered, even if it took many years.

S.G. Preston

**A Personal Prayer Tip (Modifying George Müller's):**

**Begin by Keeping a Prayer Journal Only of Prayers Already Answered**

As a new Christian, I remember praying very sporadically for about fifty different things, and in a couple of months, perhaps seeing two of these answered.

If I had recorded fifty prayers, and only seen two answered in two months, I think I would have become very discouraged.

**Gratitude and Faith**

I recommend instead: obtaining a notebook and only recording in it prayers that have already been answered. After a year or two, you will have a record that will fill you with gratitude toward God, and increase your faith as you pray.

If you can't remember exactly when you first prayed each prayer, just estimate. Or, you could still record your prayer requests in a different place.

You can always switch to George Müller's Ledger idea at any time in the future, when your faith and experience in prayer has grown.

**We Begin a 24-Hr. Prayerchain**

Count Zinzendorf and the Moravians had begun a 24-Hr. Prayerchain that lasted for 100 years!

Reading about this inspired our ministry to start our own 24-hr. Prayerchain.

Following George Müller's example, our *PrayerFoundation*™ ministry recorded each prayer request and the date we received it, when we began praying for each prayer request sent to the *24-hr. Prayerchain* that we began in 1999. Then we recorded the *Answer to Prayer* and the date we received *it*.

I have compiled many of these *prayer requests* and *answers to prayer*, with the exact dates of both, in my book, *Answers to Prayer*, which is truly  inspiring to read, illustrating as it does, God's amazing love and care for His people, through his answering of every type of *prayer request* that they have made.

### Why I Recommend This

This book, by looking at some of the greatest prayer lives in history, is meant to help, teach and inspire Christians at all stages of their prayer lives.

There is an advantage in being able to look back at over four decades of my life and remember what my prayer experiences were during that time, from the very beginning of becoming a Christian.

### Lifting Weights

Let me use exercise as an example.  You want to get in shape and be healthier, maybe lose some of that dangerous belly fat.  So you decide to work out with weights.

Wanting to learn some "tips" about what you should do, you purchase a body-building magazine.  You find the articles to be very helpful.   They are written by experts; by a Mr. Olympia, a Mr. Universe, or those in the running for it.

The magazine articles women read will be written by the female equivalents of these people.  But do most of us want to become a professional body builder?  Do most of us really have a goal of bench pressing 500 lbs.?  Probably not.

### Rather, Blessed Are Those That Hear the Word of God, and Obey It

If you read these magazines every day, even to the point where you have committed much of them to memory, would your muscles be any larger?  No, of course not.

*You have to actually do the work of lifting the weights.* You need to commit to spend enough time doing it, and you have to do it *consistently.* Day by day: over years, over decades, over a lifetime.

In the same way, *you have to actually pray.* You need to commit to spend enough time doing it, and you have to do it *consistently.* Day by day: over years, over decades, over a lifetime.

> *"But be doers of the Word, and not hearers only,*
> *deceiving yourselves.*
>
> *For if anyone is a hearer of the Word,*
> *and not a doer,*
> *they are like someone seeing their face in a mirror;*
> *they see themselves, and go their way,*
> *and immediately forget what they looked like."*

-James 1:22-24

## Avoiding Discouragement

If you begin working out with weights, you may be told to *learn correct form first* by using the bar only, with no weights at all, then with very light weights, increasing very slowly over much time.

Trying to do too much at first will only lead to very sore muscles, perhaps even an injury; either way, you won't be able to lift weights for a time. You may decide to give up.

Growing in prayer should be done similarly. Trying to do too much at first can result in disappointment, discouragement, and in your giving up.

## "Never, Never, Never Give Up" -Winston Churchill (1941)

The teaching of our Lord is that we:

> *"...ought always to pray, and not give up..."*

-Luke 15:1

Christianity is not a religion for quitters. Its commitments are for life, going on into eternity. Any growth in our prayer lives that we have experienced has not happened overnight.

Through the years, we have many times been blessed to see prayers answered only fifteen minutes after we prayed them. Usually we pray for five or six specific things every day, and see many of them answered within a week or two. But not all.

Like George Müller, some of our prayers may not be answered until after our deaths.

## A Prayer Request

We had a very specific prayer request involving an extremely traumatic incident. I do not want to describe it here, but God could easily have answered our prayer request the very next day. He didn't.

Two weeks later, it was still unanswered. Two months later, the same. But we had been expecting the answer *the very next day*. And the next. And the next.

## Expecting An Answer Every Day

A year passed, and we were still *expecting the answer every day*. Literally, every single day we were *surprised and disappointed* that the prayer had not yet been answered!

God did not answer this particular prayer until one and a half years after we began praying. It is the many quickly answered prayers that we experience, that gives us faith for those not answered immediately, but instead are long delayed.

## Consistency, Faithfulness

Only by actually praying, and committing to spend enough time praying, will we improve in our prayer lives, and we must continue doing this *consistently*. Day by day: over years, over decades, over a lifetime.

188

S.G. Preston

> *"Moreover, it is required in stewards,*
> *that they be found to be faithful."*

-1 Corinthians 4:2

I think it is worth looking once more at the words of a Desert Father quoted earlier in this book:

> *Abba Agathon answered,*
> *'I think that there is nothing more difficult*
> *than praying to God...*
>
> *In everything else a person attempts,*
> *if they don't stop,*
> *they eventually receive rest.*
>
> *But to pray,*
> *a person must strive*
> *until their very last breath."*

# 5.5  A Short History of George Müller

*"Is minic a rinne bromach gioblach
capall cumasach."*

*"An awkward colt often becomes
a beautiful horse."*

-Old Gaelic Saying

**Arrested and Jailed**

Born in in 1805 in Prussia, a part of Germany, by age ten George Müller was thinking of various ways to steal the government money his father had responsibility for.

George's school years were years of drunkenness and immorality.  He was arrested and jailed at the age of sixteen for unpaid debts.

**Rejecting Christ Until Age Twenty**

His father determined that George should become a Pastor.  Not for any spiritual reasons, but because he thought that such a career would provide his son with a good living.

George continued in his life of sin, even while studying for the ministry.

The university had 900 Divinity students, and Müller claimed that only about nine were actually Christians.

George himself received Christ at the age of twenty.

**Refusing His Salary**

Newly married and ordained a Pastor, George *refused his salary* after discovering it was collected from *"pew-rents."*  At this time, free-will offerings were not taken in churches.  Instead, set amounts were charged to reserve certain portions of the pews.

## Living On Faith

From now on, George Müller would *"live on faith."* He discovered that the amount of money he now had to live on, was actually more than his guaranteed salary had been.

Müller began founding orphanages in Bristol, England, also establishing 117 schools and educating over 120,000 young people, along with the orphans. He also founded the *Scriptural Knowledge Institution for Home and Abroad.*

## Becoming an Evangelist at Age 70

Beginning in 1875, at an age older than when most men retire from working; from the age of 70 until age 87, George Müller had a seventeen-year ministry of worldwide Evangelism.

He placed his daughter and her husband in charge of his orphanages. Even while practicing his new ministry, George continued simultaneously to *"pray in"* all of the money needed for the thousands of children in the orphanages.

Finally retiring at age 87, and living for another six years, he went home to be with the Lord at the age of 93. His Church in Bristol had about 2,000 members at that time.

# 5.6  George Müller's Four Rules

*"Agus na damnaithe fágtha gan focal*
*glaoigh ormsa I measc na naomh."*

*"While the wicked stand confounded,*
*call me with Thy saints surrounded."*

-Old Gaelic Hymn
Originally composed in Latin
by 13th Century Franciscan,
Tommaso da Celano

**George Müller's Four Rules:**

George Müller adopted the following four rules to live by, in his Christian life:

**1.  Not to receive any fixed salary,** both because in the collecting of it there was often much that was at variance with the freewill offering with which God's service is to be maintained, and in the receiving of it a danger of placing more dependence on human sources of income than in the living God Himself.

**2.  Never to ask any human being for help,** however great the need might be, but to make his wants known to the God who had promised to care for His servants and to hear their prayer.

**3.  To take the command of Luke 12:33 literally:** *'Sell what you have and give charity,'* and never to save up money, but to spend all God entrusted to him on God's poor; on the work of His kingdom.

**4.  To take Romans 8:8, *'Owe no one anything...'* literally,** and never to be in debt for anything, but to always trust God to provide.

This mode of living was not easy at first, but Müller testified it was a blessing; bringing his soul to rest in God, and drawing it into closer union with God when inclined to backslide.

S.G. Preston

**A George Müller Prayer Tip:**

**A Life of Sin and a Prayer Life of Faith Are Not Compatible**

*"Your iniquities have made a separation between you and your God; your sins have hidden his face from you."* -Isaiah 59:2

Müller taught:

> *"For it will not do, it is not possible, to live in sin,*
> *and at the same time, by communion with God,*
> *to draw down from heaven everything one needs*
> *for the life that now is."*

John Bunyan (1628-1688), who wrote *Pilgrim's Progress* while serving nearly 12 years in prison *for his faith,* stated the same truth in this way:

> *"Prayer will make a man cease from sin,*
> *or sin will entice a man to cease from prayer."*

# 5.7 George Müller's Prayer Journal

*"Ní neart go cur le chéile."*

*"There is no strength without unity."*

-Old Gaelic Saying

———

*"...forbearing one another in love;*
*endeavoring to keep the unity of the Spirit*
*in the bond of peace.*

*There is one body, and one Spirit,*
*even as you are called in one hope of your calling;*

*one Lord, one faith, one baptism,*
*one God and Father of all,*
*who is above all, and through all,*
*and in you all."*

-Ephesians 4:2-6

## A Prayer Answered Twenty-Seven Years Later

Keeping a personal Prayer Journal that records when and how God answers your prayers, can be a real blessing in your spiritual life and growth in prayer.

I have already mentioned that George Müller used an actual two-column Journal to record his prayers.

In the left column of the page he would write down his prayer request and the date that he began praying for it. In the right-hand column he would record when it was answered, with the date.

George Müller had been praying for a certain man to accept Christ for twenty-seven years. It was later learned that the man received Christ at Müller's funeral.

S.G. Preston

## Continuing Prayer Without Giving Up

There are two things that particularly strike me about this story:

1. George Müller would not stop praying for a prayer request once he wrote it down in his Prayer Journal until it was answered.

2. George Müller did not actually see the prayer's answer himself, because Müller was no longer alive when God answered it.

## Adoniram Judson and George Müller

Adoniram Judson (1788-1850), the first Christian Missionary to Burma, and a great man of prayer, once made an amazing statement that George Müller would also have felt comfortable making:

*"I never prayed sincerely and earnestly for anything, but it came at some time;*

*no matter at how distant a day,*
*somehow, in some shape,*
*probably the least I would have devised,*
*it came."*

## E.M. Bounds and George Müller

Concerning George Müller, E.M. Bounds wrote:

*"The work of George Müller in Bristol, England,*
*was a miracle of the nineteenth century.*

*It will take the opening of the books*
*at the great judgment day*
*to disclose all he wrought*
*through prayer.*

*This godly man never asked anyone for money*
*for running expenses at his orphanage*
*where hundreds of fatherless and*
*motherless children were cared for.*

*His practice was always to ask God
for just what was needed,
and the answers which came to him
read just like a record of apostolic times.*

*He prayed for everything
and trusted implicitly to God
to supply all his needs.*

*And it is a matter of record
that never did he and the orphans
ever lack for any good thing."*

# 5.8  Two Prayer Tips from George Müller

*"He worked with his hands,*
*having heard that those who are idle, '*
*...let them not eat.'*

*And he spent what he made,*
*partly for bread, and partly on those in need.*

*He prayed constantly,*
*since he learned that it is necessary*
*to pray unceasingly in private.*

*For he paid such close attention to what was read,*
*that nothing from Scripture did he fail to take in –*
*rather he grasped everything,*
*and in him the memory took the place of books."*

-Athanasius of Alexandria (c. 296/298-373 A.D.)
Writing about Anthony of Egypt  (251-356 A.D.)

**A George Müller Prayer Tip:**

**Find a Bible Promise Relating to Your Prayer**

This Prayer Tip of George Müller is mentioned by the great evangelist R.A. Torrey:

*"One of the mightiest men of prayer*
*of the last generation*
*was George Müller of Bristol, England,*

*who in the last sixty years of his life*
*(he lived to be ninety-two or ninety-three)*

*obtained the English equivalent of $7,200,000.00*
*by prayer.*

(Note: R. A. Torrey told of the amount recorded above, $7,200,000 U.S., sometime before 1929.  Torrey lived from 1856-1928.

As has already been stated in *Section 4.4*, George Müller *"prayed in"* the equivalent of 129 million U.S. dollars in 2018 U.S. Dollars, with gold at $1,300 an ounce).

**R.A. Torrey Wrote:**

*"But George Müller never prayed for a thing
just because he wanted it,
or even just because he felt it was greatly needed
for God's work.*

*When it was laid upon George Müller's heart
to pray for anything,
he would search the Scriptures to find if there
was some promise that covered the case.*

*Sometimes he would search the Scriptures for days
before he presented his petition to God.*

*And then when he found the promise,
with his open Bible before him,
and his finger upon that promise,*

*he would plead that promise,
and so he received what he asked.
He always prayed with an open Bible before him."*

**A George Müller Prayer Tip:**

**Read & Meditate On Scripture Before Praying**

This Prayer Tip of Müller's is his discovery that after meditating on Scripture, he was more able to experience a meaningful prayer time. This truth was also expressed by the Puritan writer, William Bridge (c. 1600-1670):

*"Reading without meditation is unfruitful;
meditation without reading is hurtful;
to meditate and to read without prayer upon both
is without blessing."*

There is a very interesting comment by George Müller. He said that the first thing upon awakening, he would go to prayer, but sometimes it would take him fifteen minutes or even half an hour to get *"in the Spirit."*

Then he decided to go to the Word of God first, and to read until he was led to pray. This solved his problem.

**Best Book About George Müller**

The best book we have found about George Müller's life of prayer and faith is:

*"George Müller: Delighted in God"* by Roger Steer

**Charles Spurgeon and George Müller**

Dwight Moody once traveled all the way from America to London, just to hear the preaching of Charles Spurgeon. Charles Spurgeon made the much shorter trip from London to Bristol, just to hear the preaching of George Müller.

Spurgeon recorded his reaction to this visit and his experience of hearing Müller speak from the pulpit:

> *"Of flowers of speech he has none,*
> *and we hardly think he cares for them;*
> *but of the bread of Heaven*
> *he has abundance."*

\* \* \*

# *Answers to Prayer*
## *PrayerFoundation 24-Hr. Prayerchain*

### Jan. 23, 2002 - Prayer Request:

My 27 year-old son, Trent, living hand-to-mouth in L.A. has been on and off "speed" (mostly on) for 9 years.

Please pray that Trent will be delivered permanently from drugs, healed of his psychological wounds, and above all that he will surrender his life in service to Jesus Christ.

Thank you, and may God mightily bless your prayer ministry.

*-Rick*

### Email from Trent - Apr. 26, 2002 (3 Months Later)

Hello friends,

Wow! Freedom! It sure is a good thing. Having developed a personal relationship with Jesus about 2 & 1/2 weeks ago is even better. The love and peace I feel is like nothing that the world could give to me.

Thank you all so much for your many prayers. They worked! I just want to jump and shout for joy. In jail, I began reading the book of John. Awesome stuff!

I am so excited about my new life, and I'm so lucky my dad is a true man of God. I asked him if he will baptize me sometime next week, either in his swimming pool or at the beach. What a relief, I can leave the past behind. Amen.

*-Trent*

---

(From the book: *Answers to Prayer* by S.G. Preston)

# 6: *The Original New Monasticism*

## 6.1 9am: The Lord's Prayer

*"Someone once asked St. Anthony,*
*'What must I do to please God?'*

*The old man replied, 'Pay attention to what I tell you. Wherever you go, always have God before your eyes. Whatever you do, do it according to the testimony of the Scriptures.'*

*Some of the Brothers were not satisfied with this reply and said to him, 'Abba Anthony, we would also like a word from you.'*

*Then Monk Anthony told them, 'The Gospel says: If someone strikes you on the right cheek, turn the other to them also.' They answered, 'We cannot do that.'*

*Anthony said to them, 'If you cannot offer the other one, at least allow them to strike you on one cheek.' They replied, 'We cannot even do that.' If you cannot even do that,' said Monk Anthony, 'do not pay back the evil that you have received.'*

*The Brothers answered, 'We cannot do this either.' Then the old man said to one of his disciples, 'Prepare a little broth for them, for they are ill.*

*If you cannot do this, and you will not do that, what can I do for you? You are in need of prayer.'"*

-Sayings of the Desert Fathers

**9 a.m.**

Our monastery's Grandfather Clock strikes the Westminster Chimes, the same notes that Linda and I heard from Big Ben when we were visiting London. Nine more chimes follow, one for each hour past midnight. It is now nine o'clock in the morning.

201

This is the time of day when the daily Morning Sacrifice was offered in the Temple in Jerusalem. It is the exact time of day when our Lord was crucified.

## The Lord's Prayer

It is the time of day that God chose to pour out the Holy Spirit upon the earth on the Day of Pentecost, and bring the Christian Church to birth.

Lighting a candle and placing it in the bowl of sand placed there for that purpose, I kneel before God in our Chapel.

To the Lord I will pray extemporaneously for five or ten minutes, but first I will sing or say the prayer that our Lord taught his Disciples:

*Our Father, who art in Heaven, hallowed be Thy name.*
*Thy kingdom come, Thy will be done, on earth as it is in heaven.*
*Give us this day our daily bread, and forgive us our trespasses,*
*as we forgive those who trespass against us.*
*And lead us not into temptation, but deliver us from evil.*

*For Thine is the kingdom, and the power, and the glory:*
*forever and ever. Amen.*

-Matthew 6:9-13

## The Creed

If I have not already prayed the *Nicene Creed* earlier in the day, as is the case today, I will do so now.

Yes, this Creed is technically a profession, or confession, of faith, not a prayer. It is *the* public and private Confession of Faith of Christians.

It is the only Creed accepted by the entire undivided Christian Church: first adopted in 325 A.D., and completed in 381.A.D.

202

S.G. Preston

The *Nicene Creed* also holds the distinction of being the only Creed accepted and believed in common by all three branches of Christianity: Eastern Orthodox, Roman Catholic, and Protestant.

This Creed is actually a group of Scripture verses collected together that convey the essentials of the Christian Faith, and is based on the general *Rule of Faith* of the Apostles, that had been used throughout the entire Christian Church up until that time.

## Polycarp and the Rule of Faith

If you read various compilations of the *Rule of Faith* as recorded by Early Church Bishops like Irenaeus of Lyon (also by Tertullian, and others), you will see that it is a very similar collection of Scriptures to those that make up the later *Nicene Creed*.

Irenaeus said that he was instructed in the *Rule of Faith* of the Apostles by Polycarp, (d. 156 A.D.) who had been a disciple of the Apostle John. Polycarp was made Bishop of Smyrna (today's Izmir, Turkey) by John and others of the Apostles.

In his old age, Polycarp was arrested, and a Roman Proconsul commanded him to renounce Christ or be burned at the stake. Polycarp, before his martyrdom, answered:

> *"Eighty-six years I have been His servant,*
> *and He has done me no wrong.*
>
> *How can I blaspheme*
> *my King who saved me?"*

## Irenaeus and the Rule of Faith

In *"Against Heresies,"* written between 175 and 185 A.D., Irenaeus records portions of this *Rule of Faith*.

I have quoted below part of what he wrote concerning this, so that you can see the similarity to the *Nicene Creed*, which would not be formulated completely for another 200 years.

**Against Heresies**

*Chapter 10. Unity of the Faith of the Church Throughout the Whole World:*

*"The Church, though dispersed throughout the whole world, even to the ends of the earth, has received from the Apostles and their disciples this faith:*

(She believes) *in one God, the Father Almighty, maker of heaven and earth, and the sea, and all things that are in them;*

*and in one Christ Jesus, the Son of God, who became incarnate for our salvation;*

*and in the Holy Spirit, who proclaimed through the prophets the dispensations of God, and the advents, and the birth from a virgin, and the passion,*

*and the resurrection from the dead, and the ascension into heaven in the glory of the Father..."*

## One Lord, One Faith, One Baptism

Bishop Irenaeus is explaining that from the time of the Apostles up to the time he is writing (175-185 A.D.), *all of the individual Christian churches in the world have taught these same basic essential doctrines.*

He goes on to affirm that none of these teachings originated with the Apostles, but came from Christ.

Irenaeus goes on to say that these doctrines taught by the Apostles, that were later written down and recorded in the New Testament, are still in Irenaeus' own time, taught in every Christian church throughout the world.

And that every Christian church is in total agreement as to what they teach:

S.G. Preston

*"For the Churches*
*which have been planted in Germany*
*do not believe or hand down anything different,*

*nor do those in Spain, nor those in Gaul,*
*nor those in the east,*
*nor those in Egypt, nor those in Libya,*
*nor those which have been established*
*in the central regions of the world.*

*But as the sun, that creature of God,*
*is one and the same throughout the whole world,*

*so also the preaching of the truth*
*shines everywhere,*
*and enlightens all men that are*
*willing to come to the knowledge of the truth.*

*Nor will any one of the rulers in the Churches,*
*however highly gifted he may be*
*in point of eloquence,*
*teach doctrines different from these*
*(for no one is greater than the Master);*

*nor, on the other hand,*
*will he who is deficient in power of expression*
*inflict injury on the tradition.*

*For the faith being one and the same,*
*neither does one who is able at great length*
*to discourse regarding it,*
*make any addition to it;*

*nor does one who can say but little,*
*diminish it."*

## Augustine and the Creed

Writing sometime before 430 A.D., St. Augustine of Hippo had this to say about the *Nicene Creed*:

*"We make our own the profession of the faith
that we carry in our heart...*

*We have the universal faith in the Creed,
known to the faithful and committed to memory,*

*contained in a form of expression
as concise as has been rendered admissible
by the circumstances..."*

And we do believe that the Creed should be *prayed*.

We recommend every Christian to memorize the version that their own Church uses, or that they prefer, and to pray it every day, as we believe should also be done with *The Lord's Prayer*.

**The Venerable Bede and The Creed**

The Venerable Bede (672/673-735 A.D.), the first person to translate portions of the Bible into English, including the *Gospel of John*, writes:

*"That is why I have frequently offered translations
of both the Creed and The Lord's Prayer into English...*

*For St. Ambrose the Bishop, speaking of faith,
admonishes believers to sing the words of the Creed
each morning...*

*...has taught us to sing The Lord's Prayer more often."*

-The Venerable Bede

**The Filioque**

Different translations into English of the Nicene Creed from the original Greek use slightly different wordings, but they all convey the same meaning.

The only exception to this is the addition of the *Filioque* clause: *"and the Son"* in the Roman Catholic version of the Creed, and

S.G. Preston

which most of the historic Reformation Protestant Churches have retained.

The original Greek has:

*"And I believe in the Holy Spirit,*
*the Lord and giver of life,*
*who proceeds from the Father;"*

The latter part of this sentence of the Creed was clearly taken directly from the Gospel of John:

*"Even the Spirit of Truth,*
*who proceeds from the Father;"*

John 15:26

## The Filioque Added to the Creed

*And I believe in the Holy Spirit, the Lord and giver of life, who proceeds from the Father **and the Son;*** (in Latin: ***filioque***).

The *Nicene Creed* was approved by the Bishops from throughout the entire undivided Christian Church in 325 and 381 A.D. The *Filioque* addition was first used in Toledo, Spain in 587 A.D.

The Filioque was first used in the Church at Rome, after being arbitrarily approved by Pope Benedict VIII in 1014 A.D. at the request of King Henry II of Germany, who was in Rome for his coronation as Holy Roman Emperor. Pope Benedict owed his restoration to the Papal throne to Henry, after the Antipope Gregory had usurped it.

## The Great Schism

The addition of the Filioque clause, and the Papal claim to absolute (Judicial) authority over all Christians (including the Orthodox Communions), and Eastern Orthodoxy's rejection of both doctrinal teachings as innovations, led in 1054 A.D. to the Great Schism.

This was the splitting of Eastern Orthodoxy and Roman Catholicism into two separate Churches.

In 1054 A.D., the Patriarch of Constantinople, Michael Cerularius, was visited by Papal Legates demanding that he recognize the claim of the Church of Rome to be the head and mother of the Churches.

His refusal to do so resulted in the Legates excommunicating him and denying his title of Ecumenical Patriarch. He, in turn, excommunicated the Papal Legates, as representing the Pope and the Church of Rome.

## Removing the Filioque

The Orthodox Church has *never* had the *filioque* clause, retaining the original Greek wording of the Creed since its inception. In 1988 the Anglican Church's *Lambeth Council* recommended the removal of the *filioque* from the version of the Nicene Creed that they use in their Church Services.

When I prepared our own version's wording (mainly replacing the "thees" and "thous" from the 16th century English version with the updated English: "you"), I also omitted the added *filioque* clause.

## The Nicene Creed

I will pray the Nicene Creed by either *saying* it or *singing* it this morning (technically, we sing/chant it):

*I believe in one God:*
*The Father Almighty, Maker of heaven and earth,*
*and of all things visible and invisible.*

*And in one Lord Jesus Christ,*
*the only begotten Son of God,*

*begotten of the Father before all ages:*

*God from God, Light from Light, True God from True God;*
*begotten, not made, being of one substance with the Father;*
*through Him all things were made.*
*Who, for us all, and for our salvation, came down from Heaven,*
*and was incarnate by the Holy Spirit of the virgin Mary,*
*and was made man;*
*and was crucified also for us under Pontius Pilate.*

*He suffered and was buried; and the third day He rose again,*
*in accordance with the Scriptures;*
*and ascended into Heaven,*
*and sits at the right hand of the Father.*

*And He shall return, with glory, to judge the living and the*
*dead; His kingdom shall have no end.*
*And I believe in the Holy Spirit, the Lord and giver of life,*
*who proceeds from the Father;*
*who with the Father and the Son together*
*is worshipped and glorified;*
*who spoke by the prophets.*

*And I believe in one holy, universal, and apostolic Church.*
*I acknowledge one baptism for the remission of sins;*
*and I look for the resurrection of the dead,*
*and the life of the world to come.*
*Amen.*

# 6.2  With Christ in the School of the Desert

*"As soon as He came up out of the water,*
*He saw the heavens opened,*
*and the Spirit like a dove descending upon Him.*

*And there came a voice from heaven, saying,*
*'You are My beloved Son, in whom I am well pleased.'*

*And immediately the Spirit drove Him*
*into the wilderness.*

*And He was there in the desert forty days,*
*tempted by Satan;*
*and was among the wild beasts;*
*and the angels ministered to Him."*

-Mark 1:10-13

**Prayer in the Desert**

The desert, as it is portrayed in Scripture in the life of Moses, the life of John the Baptist, and the life of Christ, was seen in that very same way by the new monastics of the third century: to be a school of the spiritual life; a school of prayer.

Many early Christians had moved to the Egyptian desert to escape the persecution of pagan Roman Emperors.

Later, many Christians, beginning with St. Anthony the Great, decided to live in the desert to draw closer to God; following the example of Christ, when he fasted forty days in the desert wilderness of Judea.

**Words Not Found in the Bible**

**Bible**:  Did you know that the word *Bible* does not appear anywhere in the Bible?

There are other words not found in the Bible, which Christians use to describe doctrines that are taught in the Bible. These include:

**Trinity**: (Isaiah 9:6; Matthew 1:23; 3:16-17; 28:19; Luke 1:35; 3:21-22; John 1-3; 10:30; 14:16-17; Romans 14:17-18; 1 Corinthians 8:6; 2 Corinthians 1:21-22; 3:17; 13:14; Colossians 2:9)

> *"...in the Name of the Father, and of the Son,*
> *and of the Holy Spirit."*

> -Matthew 28:19

**Monotheism**: (Deuteronomy 6:4, Isaiah 43:10; 44:8; Mark 12:30).

> *"Is there a God beside me? ...I know not any."*

> -Isaiah 44:8

**Divinity**: (Psalm 139; Isaiah 43:10; 44:8; John 1:1-3; Romans 1:20).

> *"...even His eternal power and Godhead..."*

> -Romans 1:20

**Omniscience**: *All-Knowing* (Psalm 139; Job 37:15; Luke 12:7; Romans 11:33; Hebrews 4:13; 1 John 3:20).

> *"...God is greater than our heart,*
> *and knows all things."*

> -1 John 3:20

**Omnipresence**: *Present Everywhere* (Job 34:21; Psalm 11:4-5; Psalm 139; Jeremiah 23:23-24; Matthew 6:6).

*"Where shall I go from Your Spirit?*
*Or where shall I flee from Your presence?*
*If I ascend up into Heaven, You are there.*
*If I make my bed in Sheol; behold: You are there."*

-Psalms 139:7-8

**Omnipotence**: *All-Powerful, Almighty* (Job 42:1-2; Psalm 33:9; Jeremiah 32:27; Nehemiah 9:6; Luke 1:37; Colossians 1:17; Revelation 19:6).

*"For with God, nothing shall be impossible."*

-Luke 1:37

**Incarnation**: *God the Son Born as a Man: Fully Human and Fully Divine* (Isaiah 9:6; Luke 1:35; John1:1-3, 14; Romans 8:3; Galatians 4:4; Philippians 2:6-7).

*"...and the Word was God.*

*And the Word was made flesh, and dwelt among us..."*

-John 1:3,14

**Rapture**: (1 Corinthians 15:51-53; 1 Thessalonians 4:16-18).

*"Then we which are alive and remain*
*shall be caught up together with them in the clouds,*
*to meet the Lord in the air:*

*and so shall we ever be with the Lord."*

-1 Thessalonians 4:17

**Atheist**: (Psalm 14:1; Psalm 53:1).

S.G. Preston

> *"The fool has said in his heart: 'There is no God.'"*

> -Psalm 14:1

## Based On the Life of Christ

The words: *monk, monastery,* and *monasticism* also do not appear in the Bible.

Yet the idea of Christian monks historically is based upon the Gospel accounts of the lives of Christ and the Apostles, along with the lives of certain of the Old Testament prophets.

Our Lord's forty day fast in the desert wilderness of Judea was greatly inspiring to the earliest Christian monks in Egypt:

*Anthony, Pachomius, and the Desert Fathers*

The lives of Elijah and John the Baptist were also found to be particularly inspiring.

## Christian Monasticism

But the ultimate inspiration for Christian monasticism was Christ's own life as recorded in the Gospels.

Our Lord's example was of a life wholly dedicated to God, bathed in prayer and Bible study, teaching, preaching, and including the practice of spiritual disciplines such as rising early for prayer, fasting, and memorization of Scripture.

The example of a community of twelve believers under the Lordship and teaching of Jesus Christ, preparing for a future as evangelists who will preach the Good News, of course comes to us from the Gospels themselves.

## Patrick and Francis

The imitation of the example of this biblically portrayed community of Disciples would come to fruition particularly in the

213

monastic ideals and practice of two major monastic movements in history.

They are: that of the ancient Celtic missionary monks, established by the *missionary Bishop* and monk St. Patrick...

...and that of the Franciscan *Order of Friars Minor*, founded by St. Francis as a *preaching* Order, and seen in the lived Christian witness of his own life in Christ.

# 6.3 Monk Anthony of Egypt

*"I saw the snares that the Enemy*
*spreads out over the world*
*and I said, groaning,*
*'What can get through such snares?'*

*Then I heard a voice saying to me: 'Humility.'"*

Anthony of Egypt (251-356 A.D.)
*"The Father of Christian Monasticism"*

### The First Christian Monk

In the third century, hundreds of Christians fled to the deserts of Egypt to escape the intermittent persecutions of the Roman Emperors.

Anthony was the first Christian who went to live in the desert solely to be with God. Because of this, St. Anthony the Great of Egypt is considered to be the very first Christian monk.

Born in 251 A.D., he was a young man, about 18 or 20 years old, when he entered a church in his native town of Coma. His Christian parents had died six months earlier, and his inheritance had left him fairly well off.

During the reading of the Gospel, Anthony heard these words of Christ from the Gospel of Matthew:

*"If you would be perfect,*
*go and sell what you have,*
*and give to the poor,*
*and you shall have*
*treasure in heaven;*

*and come and follow me."*

-Matthew 19:21

215

## Anthony Prays

Anthony distributed his land, a fertile farm of over two hundred acres, among the townspeople. He sold all of his other possessions, and gave away the money to the poor, embarking on a solitary life of prayer in the deserts of Egypt. He lived until 356 A.D., to age 105.

## He Teaches

Although he preferred being alone with God in solitary prayer, as his fame spread, many others also began to adopt this new monastic form of life. They sought out Anthony to be their spiritual director, and received teaching from him in both word and example.

There were, in addition, many others who came out temporarily from the cities to the desert, to speak with Anthony about the things of God. Even some Greek philosophers, followers of Neo-Platonism, went out to the desert, just to debate him.

## He Denounces Error

Traveling with a group of monks to Alexandria during the Arian controversy, Anthony denounced the Arians as heretics and *"Christ-fighters."* Bishop Arius and his followers, in common with most other non-Christian cults, claimed to be the only *"true Christians"* although they denied two of the most basic Christian teachings: belief in the Trinity and belief in the Deity of Christ.

## He Visits Prisoners

During one of the waves of persecution in Egypt, Anthony again journeyed to Alexandria, where the persecution was at its worst. He traveled with a group of monks, hoping, if it was the Lord's will, to receive the crown of martyrdom, but his hope was not fulfilled. He was, however, able to visit imprisoned Christians and comfort them.

216

S.G. Preston

# 6.4 Monk Anthony & Bishop Athanasius

*"For the Lord was working with Anthony –*
*the Lord who for our sake took flesh*
*and gave the body victory over the Devil,*
*so that all who truly fight can say:*

*'Not I,*
*but the grace of God*
*which was with me'"*

-Athanasius of Alexandria (c. 293-373 A.D.) Bishop;
Author: *"On the Incarnation"* and *"The Life of Anthony"*

### Athanasius Visits Anthony

Athanasius, who at this time was serving as Bishop of Alexandria, heard about Monk Anthony, and admired him greatly; often going out into the desert to visit and speak with him.

Shortly after Anthony's death, Athanasius would write his classic work: *The Life of Anthony.*

This story of Anthony's life, written by someone who had known him personally, one of the most respected leaders in Christendom, kindled great interest in this new Christian Monasticism movement.

It would soon spread throughout the entire known world of the Roman Empire, and even beyond.

### Constantine

Anthony's fame even reached Emperor Constantine, who wrote to him, praising Anthony's life, and asking for prayer.

The monks were very excited and happy about Anthony receiving this letter. However, Anthony ignored it, saying:

217

*"The books of God,*
*the King of Kings and the Lord of Lords,*
*command us every day;*
*but we do not heed what they tell us,*
*and we turn our backs on them."*

The monastic Brothers would not relent, but continued telling Anthony how much the Emperor loved the Church. Anthony finally consented to write an answering letter, saying that he would pray for the Emperor, and for the peace and safety of the Empire and the Church.

**An Anthony of Egypt Prayer Tip:**

**Conform to God and Give Thanks in All Things**

Anthony of Egypt taught this about prayer:

*"The truly intelligent man*
*pursues one sole objective:*
*to obey and conform to the God of all.*

*With this single aim in view,*
*he disciplines his soul,*
*and whatever he may encounter*
*in the course of his life,*

*he gives thanks to God*
*for the compass and depth*
*of His providential ordering*
*of all things."*

**Walking Into the Desert**

As time went on, an ever-growing number of people arrived to visit Anthony. His response was to walk for three days deep into the desert, just so he could be alone with God.

# 6.5  Monk Pachomius of Egypt

*"O God, Creator of heaven and earth,
cast on me an eye of pity;
deliver me from my miseries.*

*Teach me the true way of pleasing You,
and it shall be the whole employment,
the most earnest study of my life
to serve You, and to do Your will."*

-A Prayer of Pachomius

### Pachomius Receives Christ

Pachomius (290-346 A.D.) was a pagan conscripted by the Roman Army. He was sent, with others in the same situation, on a ship to Alexandria, Egypt. Along the way, they stopped temporarily at the Egyptian city of Latopolis.

The conscripts were imprisoned to prevent any attempt to escape. In Latopolis, Christians had the practice of bringing food and drink to prisoners. It was Pachomius' first experience of Christianity, and seeing this living out of the Gospel teachings in daily life, he became convinced to receive Christ in his own life.

### Pachomius Founds the First Monastery

The first Christian monks were what we would call religious hermits; our English word *hermit* coming from the Greek word: *eremite.*

It was Pachomius, a contemporary of Anthony, who formed the first organized monastic *community* (*cenobites*). When it grew too large, he founded six more monasteries.

The number of monks in his communities increased to total nearly seven thousand.

## The First Women's Monastic Community

There had previously existed many early monastic communities not formally organized, made up of individual *eremitic* hermit-type monks who of their own accord would meet together weekly for religious services, including Communion.

These two types of Christian monasticism, *cenobitic* and *eremitic*, have remained in existence for the past 1,700 years. Pachomius was also the first to organize a women's monastic community. He built a Convent Monastery in which a number of religious women lived with his sister, Maria.

## Greek Speaking

Our English word *monk* comes from the Greek word *monakhós,* meaning: *alone, single, solitary.* Christians in Egypt in the fourth century were members of a Greek speaking population.

The Hebrew Old Testament had been translated into the Greek *Septuagint* Old Testament even before Christ was born. The books of the New Testament were written in Greek.

## Replaced by Latin

The entire Early Church had spoken Greek, and Christians in the Eastern half of the Empire still did, but three hundred years after the time of the Apostles, most Christians in the Western Roman Empire could only speak Latin.

Even St. Augustine, an educated Roman citizen, a Bishop in the Church, and the author of at least fifty books, could not read or write Greek.

## Jerome and Augustine

A monk in the Holy Land named Jerome (c. 347-419/420), is considered to be the most learned of the Latin Fathers. He translated the Bible from the Greek *Septuagint* into Latin.

Jerome was also knowledgeable in Hebrew. His translation of the Scriptures is known as the *Latin Vulgate*. It would remain the primary version of the Bible in Western Europe for over 1,000 years, until the Protestant Reformation in the early 1500's.

Augustine and Jerome were friends, and they often corresponded with each other. Jerome made fun of Augustine's inability to read the Scriptures in Greek and Hebrew.

## The Rule of Pachomius

Around 404 A.D., Jerome would also translate *The Rule of Pachomius* into Latin.

One part of this Rule states that everyone in the monastery was to know by heart at least the New Testament and the Psalms.

# 6.6  Monk Basil the Great

*"I want creation to penetrate you
with so much admiration
that everywhere,
wherever you may be,
the least plant may bring to you
the clear remembrance
of the Creator.*

*If you see the grass of the fields,
think of human nature,
and remember the comparison
of the wise Isaiah:*

*'All flesh is grass,
and all the goodliness thereof
is as the flower of the field.'"*

-Basil the Great (329-379 A.D.)
Bishop, Theologian, Cappadocian Father
Writing in his book: *The Hexameron*

## Raised in a Christian Family

Basil the Great, like Anthony of Egypt before him, began his Christian ministry by giving away his possessions.

Basil's family was both wealthy and strongly Christian. Some of his ancestors had become martyrs for the Christian faith.

Basil was the brother of Gregory of Nyssa, and the friend of Gregory of Nazianzus.

Together all three are known as the *Cappadocian Fathers*. Cappadocia is located in what is today the country of Turkey. Basil went to live as a monk in the strangely shaped mountains of Cappadocia, where Christians had fled to escape persecution.

S.G. Preston

## A Universal Problem

Basil was happy to have escaped the multitude of sinful temptations found in the city. But he would grow to learn that the problem of sin ultimately resided within himself; in his own fleshly sinful nature. This universal problem is expressed well by the popular saying:

*"No matter where you go, there you are."*

## Seeking Solitude

Basil wrote about his love of solitude and of God's natural creation, to his friend Gregory of Nazianzus. These themes are to be found repeatedly in many monastic movements.

They can be found in that of the ancient Celtic monks, through Francis of Assisi, to our own contemporary practice of *Evangelical New Monasticism*, as contemporary *Celtic Lay Monks*. Basil wrote:

*"God has shown me a region*
*which exactly suits my mode of life;*
*it is, in truth,*
*what in our happy jesting*
*we often wished for.*

*What imagination showed us in the distance,*
*that I now see before me.*

*A high mountain covered with thick forest,*
*is watered towards the north*
*by fresh perennial streams.*

*At the foot of the mountain,*
*a wide plain spreads out,*
*made fruitful by the mists that water it.*

*The surrounding forest,*
*in which many varieties of trees crowd together,*
*shuts me off like a strong castle.*

*This wilderness is bounded by two deep ravines.*

*On one side the stream,*
*where it rushes foaming down from the mountain,*
*forms a barrier hard to cross;*
*on the other, a broad ridge obstructs approach.*

*My hut is so placed upon the summit,*
*that I overlook the broad plain,*
*as well as the whole course of the Iris,*
*which is more beautiful and copious*
*than the Strymon near Amphipolis.*

*The river of my wilderness,*
*more rapid than any other that I know,*
*breaks upon the wall of projecting rock,*
*and rolls foaming into the abyss;*

*to the mountain traveler,*
*a charming, wonderful sight;*
*to the natives, profitable for its abundant fisheries.*

*Shall I describe to you the fertilizing vapors*
*that rise from the moistened earth,*
*the cool air that rises from*
*the moving mirror of the water?*

*Shall I tell of the lovely singing of the birds*
*and the richness of blooming plants?*
*What delights me above all is the silent repose of the place.*

*It is only now and then visited by huntsmen;*
*for my wilderness nourishes deer*
*and herds of wild goats, not bears and wolves.*

*How would I exchange a place with him?*
*Alcmaeon, after he had found the Echinades,*
*wished to wander no further.*

*Silent solitude is the beginning*
*of purification of the soul.*

*For the mind; if it is not disturbed from without,*
*and does not lose itself*
*through the senses in the world;*
*withdraws into itself, and rises to thoughts of God.*

*I have well forsaken my residence in the city*
*as a source of a thousand evils,*
*but I have not been able to forsake myself.*

*I am like a man who, unaccustomed to the sea,*
*becomes seasick, and gets out of the large ship,*
*because it rocks more, into a small skiff,*
*but still even there keeps the dizziness and nausea.*

*So it is with me;*
*for while I carry about with me*
*the passions which dwell in me,*
*I am everywhere tormented*
*with the same restlessness,*

*so that I really get not much help*
*from this solitude."*

## Basil Writes a Monastic Rule

Influenced by Pachomius, who had written the very first Rule for a *cenobitic* monastic community, Basil founded several of this new communal type of monastery in Cappadocia.

Basil would write his own Rule of monastic life for these new monks. He wrote both a *Short Rule* and a *Long Rule*.

The Rules of Pachomius and Basil have remained the basic foundation of monastic life for all Eastern Orthodox monks for the past 1,600 years.

# 6.7 Monk Benedict of Nursia

*"...a little Rule for beginners...*
*nothing harsh, nothing burdensome..."*

-St. Benedict (480-547 A.D.)
*"The Father of Western Monasticism"*

## Renouncing the World

Only one year after the death of Basil, Benedict was born in Nursia, Italy. He would use Basil the Great's *Long Rule* and *Short Rule* as the basis for his own monastic Rule: *The Rule of St. Benedict.*

Except for the followers of the *Augustinian* Order, this would become the Rule adopted by all of the later Roman Catholic Orders during the Middle Ages, continuing up through today.

Benedict lived in Italy at a time when the Western Roman Empire had disintegrated. The city of Rome had fallen to barbarians in 476 A.D., just four years before Benedict was born.

Disgusted by the paganism all around him, the young Benedict renounced the world and began living in a cave near Subiaco.

## Monte Cassino

Benedict would become the founder of a monastery on the mountain of Monte Cassino. It would become the oldest continuously inhabited monastery in Europe.

During WWII, the Nazis used it as a fortification, thinking that the Allies would never destroy such an important historical and religious structure. The American army, liberating Italy and heading north to Berlin, did have a policy of not bombing historic structures.

However, because the Nazis had occupied the monastery in order to stop the Allied advance into mainland Europe toward Germany, the Allies felt that they had no choice.

They leveled it to the ground.

The Benedictine monks who had lived there, returning at the end of the war, merely said that they had already built it once before, and that they would now build it again.

## 6.8  Monk Augustine of Hippo

*"Bidh an t-ubhal as fhearr
air a'mheangan as airde."*

*"The best apple is on
the highest bough."*

-Old Gaelic Saying

———

*"My heart was restless,
until it found its rest in Thee."*

-St. Augustine of Hippo  (354-430 A.D.)
Bishop, Theologian, Church Father

### 374 A.D.: Augustine's Conversion to Christianity

Bishop Augustine, the author of the classic Christian book, *The City of God*, also wrote an even more popular autobiographical work, *The Confessions*. It is only the second autobiography ever written in the West, the first being *"The Life"* by Flavius Josephus, in 100 A.D.

Raised by a Christian mother, Monica, and a pagan father, Augustine did not become a Christian until adulthood. In *The Confessions*, Augustine tells of his conversion to Christianity in 374 A.D.

He and a friend had only moments before been reading Athanasius' new book, *"The Life of Anthony."*

### Thinking Our Thoughts to God

In his later Christian writings, Augustine would often address his thoughts directly to God. Concerning his previous sinful life, he wrote:

228

*"I became evil for no reason.*
*I had no motive for my wickedness*
*except wickedness itself.*

*It was foul, and I loved it.*
*I loved the self-destruction.*

*I loved my fall;*
*not the object for which I had fallen,*
*but my fall itself.*

*My depraved soul leaped down*
*from your firmament to ruin.*

*I was seeking not to gain anything*
*by shameful means,*
*but shame for its own sake."*

In 388 A.D., Augustine and a few Christian friends founded the *Servei Dei* (*Servants of God*) monastic Order. Centuries later it would be re-founded as the *Augustinian* Order, the oldest monastic Fraternity in the West.

### Life With Christ Contrasted to Life Separated From Christ

It is all Christ. Christ is humanity's only *Way* to God. Christ our *Way* is *Truth*: *"the Life found only in God."*

When a person dies and stands before God, all of the fantasy *untruths* now found in this world will be stripped away, and immediately vanish like the unstable fictions (lies) that they actually are.

Humanity's unending attempts to get to God by self-effort have always been futile, for humanity is separated from God by sin. In his many books, Augustine often compared and contrasted life with Christ, to life separated from Christ:

*"The good man, though a slave, is free.*
*The wicked, though he reigns,*

229

*is a slave, and not the slave of a single man,*
*but--what is worst—*
*the slave of as many masters*
*as he has vices."*

## A Monk for Life

Monk Augustine, as we have pointed out earlier, would go on to become a Bishop in North Africa, of the Roman city of Hippo Regius (founded by Phoenicians, it is today's Annaba, Algeria).

Augustine authored at least 50 books, and became recognized as *the* Theologian of the Western Church, by both Roman Catholics and by Protestant Reformers. He would remain a monk for the rest of his life.

## A Love Poem to God

Augustine wrote:

*"You called, and cried out loud,*
*and shattered my deafness.*

*You were radiant and resplendent.*
*You put to flight my blindness.*

*You were fragrant, and I drew in my breath...*
*I tasted You and I feel but hunger*
*and thirst for You.*

*You touched me, and I am set on fire*
*to attain the peace*
*which is Yours."*

# 6.9 Monk John Chrysostom

*"I do not believe in the salvation of anyone*
*who does not try to save others."*

-John Chrysostom (349-c. 407 A.D.)
Monk, Patriarch (Archbishop) of Constantinople

## John Becomes a Christian

John Chrysostom was raised by a widowed pagan mother. She secured training for him with a famous pagan rhetorician and lawyer. At first preparing for a law career, John decided to abandon law, and instead serve the Savior. He received baptism at age twenty-three.

John then joined himself to a monastery and received training to be ordained a priest. His great speaking skills gained him fame throughout the entire Christian world. His only desire was to live the life of a simple monk, but instead he was made Archbishop of Constantinople, against his choice.

## The Divine Liturgy of St. John Chrysostom

John was known for his eloquent preaching and public speaking, and for denouncing abuse of authority by the political and ecclesiastical hierarchies of his time. *Chrysostom* means *"Golden Mouth,"* and was a title given him after his death.

*The Divine Liturgy of St. John Chrysostom* has been in continuous use for 1,600 years in the Eastern Orthodox Church, since the fifth century.

## Chrysostom and Basil

It is actually a revision and simplification of an earlier and much longer liturgy: that of Basil the Great. Chrysostom's liturgy usually lasts about two hours, including the *Homily*: a *short Sermon*; these days usually only fifteen or twenty minutes long.

John's own teaching Homilies lasted between thirty minutes and two hours. In Basil's time the *previous* liturgy was even longer, and Basil had already shortened it considerably.

*The Divine Liturgy of St. James is often celebrated in the Eastern Orthodox Church on the Feast of St. James* (October 23). *The Divine Liturgy of St. Basil the Great* is observed ten times per year. *The Divine Liturgy of St. John Chrysostom* is used in worship every Sunday the rest of the year.

## Chrysostom and Jerome

Chrysostom shortened St. Basil's liturgy because John thought that more time should be spent preaching God's Word. John believed that:

> *"The lack of scriptural knowledge
> is the source of all evils in the Church."*

Chrysostom, Augustine, and Jerome were contemporaries; all lived in the 4th century. John's teaching about lack of scriptural knowledge is complimented very nicely by the teaching of Jerome, who wrote:

> *"Ignorance of the Scriptures
> is ignorance of Christ."*

## A John Chrysostom Prayer Truth:

## Prayer Is the Light of the Soul

In common with the later Irish Celtic monks and the even later Franciscans, John Chrysostom's monasticism found its expression in an intense burden for evangelism, as the outgrowth of his prayer life. About prayer, John wrote:

S.G. Preston

*"Blazing fire has been overcome by potent praying.*
*Raging lions have been subdued,*
*anarchy defeated;*
*war has been turned to peace,*
*the very weather changed.*

*Demons have been cast out, death overruled;*
*Heaven's Gates opened,*
*illnesses healed,*
*deceptions exposed.*

*Cities have been delivered from their destruction,*
*the Sun has been stopped still in the sky;*
*even thunder and lightning have ceased.*

*Prayer is all-sufficient, of unlimited value,*
*a treasure that never fails.*
*It is a cloudless sky, with no storm on the horizon.*

*It is the beginning and ending,*
*springing up overflowing*
*with blessings one-thousand-fold."*

———

*"Prayer is the light of the soul,*
*giving us true knowledge of God.*

*It is a link mediating between God and man.*

*Through prayer the soul*
*is carried up to heaven,*
*and in a marvelous way*
*embraces the Lord.*

*This meeting is like that of an infant*
*crying on its mother,*
*and seeking the best of milk.*

*The soul longs for its own needs,*
*and what it receives is better than*
*anything to be seen in the world."*

## Speaking Truth to Power

*"If the world hates you,*
*know that it hated Me*
*before it hated you.*

*If you were of the world,*
*the world would love its own.*

*Because you are*
*not of the world,*
*but I have chosen you*
*out of the world,*
*therefore the world hates you…*

*If they have persecuted Me,*
*they will also persecute you…"*

-John 15:18-20

## Forced to March Until Death

John seemed to be liked and appreciated by everyone except the Emperor and the Empress Eudoxia, who he had criticized in some of his sermons.

Offending the Emperor, and more especially the Empress, by his condemnation of their sins, John was ordered to be force-marched by an Imperial guard across the Greek peninsula.

The intent from the beginning was that he should suffer much and die. Until he was finally released in death, John was marched every day, given little food, and experienced much hardship and sickness in cold and rainy weather.

Even after his death, his remains were not to be left in peace. John's relics were looted from the city of Constantinople by Crusaders in 1204 A.D., and taken to Rome.

His bones were finally returned to Istanbul (formerly, Constantinople) in 2004 by Pope John Paul II, eight hundred years later.

S.G. Preston

## Doctors of the Church

What exactly are *Doctors of the Church?* Who were they?

John Chrysostom is revered in both the Eastern Orthodox and Roman Catholic Churches as one of the great *Doctors* of the Eastern Church. It is a title that has been given to eight of the foremost and renowned *Teachers* of Holy Scripture in the Early Church.

The Eastern Church recognizes *three* great Doctors of the Church, which it calls: *The Three Hierarchs.* *Hierarchs* is the Eastern Orthodox term for Archbishops. They are:

*John Chrysostom, Basil the Great,*
*and Gregory Nazianzus.*

## Gregory Nazianzus

Gregory taught:

*"As a fish cannot swim*
*without water,*
*and as a bird cannot fly*
*without air,*

*so a Christian cannot advance*
*a single step*
*without Christ."*

*"Remember God more often*
*than you breathe."*

The Roman Catholic Church adds Athanasius to this Eastern Orthodox Church list to make four; to have a more similar comparison to those they consider to be the four great Doctors of the Western Church:

*Ambrose, Augustine, Jerome,*
*and Gregory the Great.*

## Ambrose of Milan

*"It is a better thing to save souls for the Lord
than to save treasures.*

*He who sent forth His Apostles without gold,
had not need of gold to form His Church.*

*The Church possesses gold,
not to hoard,
but to scatter abroad
and come to the aid of the unfortunate."*

-Ambrose of Milan (c. 340-397)

Bishop Ambrose and John Chrysostom had much in common. Both were very sound in Doctrine and are recognized as Doctors of the Church.

Both had the same burning desire to save souls.

## Excommunicating the Emperor

Like John Chrysostom, Ambrose stood up for his faith by standing up to an Emperor. Bishop Ambrose is known for excommunicating Emperor Theodosius I for the massacre in 390 A.D. of 7,000 people in Thessalonica. Ambrose stated:

*"The Emperor is in the Church,
not above the Church."*

Ambrose had originally been a well-respected politician, the Governor of Liguria and Emilia; when, like Augustine and John Chrysostom, against his wishes, he was elected Bishop of Milan in 374 A.D.

He became a great opponent of the Arian heresy, even writing several books against their errors.

**When in Rome**

Bishop Ambrose is well known for being the Pastor and Mentor of St. Augustine. He is not as well known for originating the famous proverb:

*"When in Rome, do as the Romans do."*

These were not his exact words. This often repeated saying is derived from advice the Bishop gave to Augustine, who wrote in a letter to his son, Januarius:

*"My mother, having joined me at Milan,*
*found that the church there*
*did not fast on Saturdays, as at Rome,*
*and was at a loss as to what to do.*

*I consulted St. Ambrose,*
*of holy memory, who replied,*
*'When I am at Rome, I fast on a Saturday;*
*when I am at Milan I do not.*

*Do the same.*
*Follow the custom of the church where you are."*

-Ambrose of Milan
Recorded by Augustine of Hippo
*Epistle to Januarius* (Letter 53, Chapter 2)

**Prayer of Repentance**

A prayer of Ambrose was:

*"Forget not, O Lord,*
*that I am one of those You have created,*
*and with Your own blood have redeemed.*

*I repent of my sins:*
*I will strive to amend my ways."*

## Let Us Return to John Chrysostom

John Chrysostom once said:

*"If but ten of us lead a holy life,*
*we shall kindle a fire*
*which shall light up the entire city."*

## God Revealed in Creation

Like so many monastics throughout history, Chrysostom waxed eloquent about God's revelation of Himself in His Creation:

*"If you see a splendid building,*
*and the view of its colonnades transports you,*
*look quickly at the vault of the heavens*
*and the open fields,*
*on which the flocks are feeding*
*on the shore of the sea.*

*Who does not despise every creation of art;*
*when in the silence of the heart,*
*he early wonders at the rising sun,*
*as it pours its golden, crocus-yellow light*
*over the horizon?*

*When, resting at a spring in deep grass,*
*or under the dark shade of thick trees,*
*he feeds his eyes upon the dim*
*vanishing distance?"*

## A John Chrysostom Prayer Tip:

## Prayer Brings Joy

John taught:

*"Prayer is the place of refuge for every worry,*
*a foundation for cheerfulness,*

238

S.G. Preston

*a source of constant happiness,*
*a protection against sadness."*

———

*"There is nothing more worthwhile*
*than to pray to God and converse with Him,*
*for prayer unites us with God*
*as His companions."*

———

*"If we are generous in giving time to prayer,*
*we will experience its benefits*
*throughout our life."*

**A John Chrysostom Prayer Truth**

**Prayer Is Desire for God, Given Us by God's Grace**

John Chrysostom's extensive preaching covers the entire range of *Scripture*, but his teaching on prayer is especially inspiring:

*"Prayer is a precious way*
*of communicating with God,*
*it gladdens the soul*
*and gives repose to its affections.*

*You should not think of prayer*
*as being a matter of words.*

*It is a desire for God,*
*an indescribable devotion;*
*not of human origin,*
*but the gift of God's grace."*

# 6.10 Monk Martin of Tours

*"Lord, if your people
need me,
I will not refuse
the work.
Your will be done."*

-Martin of Tours
(c. 316-367 A.D.)
When acclaimed
Bishop of Tours,
an Office he did not desire.

## Martin of Tours

We do not know Martin's exact birthdate. We do know that he was born in what is now Hungary, and grew up in northern Italy.

Christianity was not made legal in the Roman Empire until 313 A.D., perhaps only three years before Martin was born.

Raised by pagan parents, Martin accepted the Lord when he was ten. He would later lead his mother to Christ, but not his father.

## Forced to Join the Roman Legions

Because his father was an Officer in the Roman Army's Cavalry, Martin was required by law to also join the Cavalry at the age of fifteen.

While in active service as a Cavalry Officer, Martin experienced what would become the most repeated story about his life. He was at the gates of the city of Amiens with his soldiers, when he met a beggar dressed in only a few rags.

Martin impulsively drew his sword and cut his own military cloak in half, sharing it with the beggar.

## Martin's Dream

That night Martin dreamed of Jesus, who in the dream was wearing the half-cloak that Martin had given away. In his dream Martin heard Jesus say to the angels:

*"Here is Martin,*
*the Roman soldier who is not baptized.*
*He has clothed Me."*

Martin was then 18 years old; he first became a Catechumen (a Christian convert preparing for baptism) and then was baptized.

## Refusing to Fight

Martin served in the military for another two years until, just before a battle with the Gauls in 336 A.D., near today's city of Worms, Germany, he determined that his faith prohibited him from fighting, saying:

*"I am a soldier of Christ.*
*I cannot fight."*

## Released from Service

He was charged with cowardice and jailed, but in response, he volunteered to go unarmed before the enemy, at the front of the Roman troops. His superiors planned to take Martin up on his offer, but before they could, the invaders sued for peace, the battle never occurred, and he was released from military service.

(Note: Martin Luther was baptized on St. Martin of Tours' day, November 11th, and because of this was given the first name of Martin.

In 1521, Luther refused to recant at the Diet of Worms, the same city near which the man he was named for, had refused to fight.)

**Timeline of the Spread of Monasticism in Western Europe:**

**Hilary of Poitiers and Martin of Tours**

Martin declared his vocation as a monk, and made his way to the city of Tours. There he became a disciple of Hilary of Poitiers, a chief proponent of Trinitarian Christianity; opposing the Arianism of the barbarian Visigoths.

In 361 A.D., Martin founded Liguge Monastery. In 371 A.D., he was acclaimed Bishop of Tours by the Christians of that city.

**Martin and Ambrose**

Martin was made Bishop against his will, as had happened with John Chrysostom and Ambrose of Milan.

This would also be the case with Augustine of Hippo only twenty-five years later, in 396 A. D. Martin and Ambrose were contemporaries, and knew each other.

Only a year after Founding Liguge, Martin would Found, in 372 A.D., a second monastery at Marmoutier.

**Forced to Flee for His Life**

During this time, the Roman province of Gaul (today's France) was still inhabited by the people of that name, a Celtic people who followed the Druidic religion and its priests.

Gaul was also inhabited by another barbarian tribe, the Visigoths, who had been converted to the Arian heresy after migrating from central Europe.

Greatly devoted to evangelism, Martin led many to Christ. In this he was fiercely opposed by both Druids and Arians. Even the Roman Emperor at this time was an Arian.

Martin was forced to flee for his life from Arian persecution, and went to live as a hermit monk on an island off of the Italian coast.

S.G. Preston

## 397 A.D. - Ninian of Caledonia

Ninian trained at Martin's Marmoutier Monastery as a monk, before becoming the first missionary to Caledonia (the Roman name for Scotland). He founded Whithorn Monastery (*Candida Casa,* meaning: *White House*) there in 397 A.D.

## 410 A.D. - Honoratus of Lerins

Lerins Monastery (Lerins Abbey) was founded on what is now known as the island of Saint-Honorat, one of the Lerins Islands near the southern coast of France. Its Founder was named Honoratus.

He had been Archbishop of Amiens, the city where Martin of Tours had shared his cloak with the beggar, and retired as a monk to one of the uninhabited Lerins Islands in 410 A.D. Lerins Monastery was home and training school to two monks who would later become quite famous: St. Vincent of Lerins, and St. Patrick of Armagh.

## 422 A.D. - Germaine of Auxerre

A new monastery would be founded by Germaine at Auxerre, in Gaul, in 422 A.D. This was one of two monasteries; the other being Honoratus' monastery at Lerins; that a runaway slave named Patrick would train at, before receiving a call from God three times in dreams, to go as a missionary to Ireland.

## 529 A.D. - Benedict of Nursia

Benedict would not found his first monastery, near Subiaco, Italy, until 529 A.D. When he later climbed the mountain of Monte Cassino to establish a second monastery, he found a Greek temple to Apollo built atop the summit, where the local idolatrous inhabitants worshipped.

Benedict's first act was to smash the idol: a statue of Apollo. Next, he built a small Oratory (Chapel) there, and dedicated it to Martin of Tours.

## Monasteries as Mission Stations

From Martin of Tours until Benedict of Nursia, 336-529 A.D., nearly 200 years had passed. This was a very productive time period in fulfilling Christ's *Great Commission.*

Monasteries were founded either as mission stations to convert the local pagan inhabitants, or as schools to train monks, who would then be sent out as missionaries to take the Gospel where it had never been heard before.

## 432 A.D. - St. Patrick

Celtic Christianity could be considered the *"second wave"* of the *original* New Monasticism."

These monastic practices were also established in Ireland by St. Patrick, who returned there as a missionary in 432 A.D. They would continue in Ireland until the suppression of the Celtic Church and the end of the historic Celtic Christian Era at the Synod of Cashel in 1172 A.D. The Celtic Christian Era comprises 740 years of missionary monks evangelizing Ireland and Continental Europe.

## 1209 A.D. – St. Francis

Only forty years after Ireland's Synod of Cashel, there would be one more attempt to evangelize Europe by another, who, like Martin of Tours, was himself a former soldier.

In 1209 A.D., he founded a new preaching Order of monastics.

A full-time Order for men, the *Order of Friars Minor;* a second full-time Order for women, the *Order of St. Clare;* and a *Third Order* for single people and married couples who chose to remain in their own homes, with jobs, careers, children.

You might even call it the *"third wave"* of the *original* New Monasticism.

S.G. Preston

Like the original introduction of Christianity to the world by Christ and the Apostles, it was accomplished without any promotion or advertising, and without any attempts at fund-raising.

## One Solitary Life

It was accomplished solely by *one man*, whose only *"program"* was *to attempt to imitate Christ in his own life*. The fact that *one solitary life* can have an effect on the world...even *change the world*, is God's message throughout Scripture.

It was God's message in the Old and New Testaments. It was God's message in Christ. It was God's message in the life Martin Luther and in the life of St. Francis. It is God's message today. Isaiah 6:8 records:

> *"And I heard the voice of the LORD saying,*
> *'Who shall I send, and who will go for Us?'*
>
> *Then I said,*
> *'Here I am; send me.'"*

* * * * *

# If You Have Been Blessed In Any Way, By Anything In This Book

Or have just enjoyed it, would you be kind enough to please leave a Review for this book at *Amazon Books?* Just Google: *Prayer as a Total Lifestyle* and click on the Book Cover.

Thank you, and may God continue to richly bless you as you serve Him!

———

**If You Would Like to Subscribe** to our E-Newsletter and be informed when New Books are published: eBooks, Print Books, and Audiobooks, just send the word…

*Subscribe* to: monks@prayerfoundation.org

\* \* \*

# About the Author

S.G. Preston and his wife Linda, Evangelical Protestants, founded the *PrayerFoundation*™ and its associated Lay Monastic order, the *Knights of Prayer*™ in 1999.  It was the first Evangelical Monastic Order on the Internet, and remained the only one for the next four years.  They live in the beautiful Pacific Northwest with four cats and a Scottish Terrier named Hermiston, where they enjoy prayer and Bible study, hiking (with Hermiston), camping, cycling, sailing, skiing, and horseback riding.

# *S.G. Preston Ministries* ™

(List of Ministries and Contact Information):

**Post Office Mail:** P.O. Box 873914, Vancouver, WA 98687
**Email:** *monks@prayerfoundation.org*

*The Prayer Foundation* (Founded 1999*) PrayerFoundation* ™
International, Interdenominational, Evangelical.

**Original Website:** *www.prayerfoundation.org* (Went Online 1999)
*The Prayer Foundation*
(Over 1,300 Webpages of *Prayer Teaching & Resources*
*from All Christian Communions and Eras*).

**New Website:** *www.prayerfoundation.net*
*PrayerFoundation Lay Monks* ™ (Went Online 2020).

*Knights of Prayer Lay Monks* ™ (Founded 1999).
Married or Single, remaining in own jobs, careers, churches.
Lay Monks Registered from all 50 States and 47 Countries.

Publishing: *PrayerFoundation Press* ™ (Founded 2018).

S.G. Preston

# *Recommended Books:*

**In Bold: Must Read** (or: **Must Listen To** on Audiobook if available).
*In Italics*: *Highly Recommended*
Not in Italics: Recommended.

## Prayer:

**"*Power Through Prayer*" by E.M. Bounds**
**"*The Kneeling Christian*" (Anonymous)**
**"*Hudson Taylor's Spiritual Secret*" by Dr. Taylor**
**"*George Muller: Delighted in God*" by Roger Steer**

*"The Practice of the Presence of God" by Brother Lawrence*
*"Prayer" by O. Hallesby*
*"Psalms: The Prayer Book of the Bible" by Dietrich Bonhoeffer*

(All other books on prayer by E.M. Bounds)
*"The Path of Celtic Prayer" by Calvin Miller*
*"The Path of Prayer" by Samuel Chadwick*
*"The Power of Prayer" by R.A. Torrey*
*"With Christ in the School of Prayer"* by Andrew Murray
*"The Life and Diary of David Brainerd"* Edited by Jonathan Edwards
(Scholarly)

## Basic Christian Teaching:

**"*Mere Christianity*" by C.S. Lewis**
**"*Knowing God*" by J.I. Packer**

*"Growing in Christ" by J.I. Packer*
*"God Wrote a Book" by James McDonald*
*"Spiritual Disciplines for the Christian Life"* by Donald S. Whitney

*"Christ, Baptism and the Lord's Supper: Recovering the Sacraments for Evangelicals"* by Leonard Vander Zee

*"The Confessions"* by St. Augustine

*"On the Incarnation"* by St. Athanasius of Alexandria  (Scholarly)

*"The Knowledge of the Holy"* by A.W. Tozer

## Christian Life:

*"L'Abri"* by **Edith Schaeffer** (Autobiography)

*"Desiring God"* by **John Piper** (Teaching)

*"E.M. Bounds: Man of Prayer"* by **Lyle Dorsett** (Biography)

"St. Francis of Assisi" by Omer Englebert (Biography)

## Daily Devotional:

*"The Imitation of Christ"* by Thomas à Kempis

## Celtic Christianity / Celtic Monasticism:

*"How the Irish Saved Civilization"* by **Thomas Cahill** (second half of book only, from *St. Patrick* on: History of Irish Celtic Monasticism) (Note: This is a book written by a Secular Author)

*"Sun Dancing"* by **Geoffrey Moorhouse** (History of Monks at Skellig Michael) (Note: This is a book written by a Secular Author)

*"Celtic Christianity: Yesterday, Today, and for the Future"* by Paul D.J. Arblaster

*"Flame in My Heart: St Aidan for Today"* by David Adam

*"The Path of Celtic Prayer"* by Calvin Miller

*"Thin Places: An Evangelical Journey into Celtic Christianity"* by Tracy Balzer

*"The Celtic Way of Evangelism"* by George G. Hunter III

S.G. Preston

## Early Church Teaching and Practice:

*"Reading Scripture with the Church Fathers"* by **Christopher A. Hall**

*"Learning Theology with the Church Fathers"* by **Christopher A. Hall**

*"Worshipping with the Church Fathers"* by **Christopher A. Hall**

*"Living Wisely with the Church Fathers"* by **Christopher A. Hall**

*"Ancient-Future Faith"* by **Robert E. Webber**

*"Ancient-Future Worship"* by **Robert E. Webber**

*"Ancient-Future Time"* by **Robert E. Webber**

*"The Sign of the Cross: The Gesture, the Mystery, the History"* by Andreas Andreopoulos

*"Getting to Know the Church Fathers: An Evangelical Introduction"* by Bryan Litfin

*"Beyond Smells and Bells: The Wonder and Power of Christian Liturgy"* by Mark Galli

*"A New Song for an Old World: Musical Thought, Early Church"* by Calvin R. Stapert

*"Evangelicals and Nicene Faith: Reclaiming the Apostolic Witness"* Editor, Timothy George

*"Retrieving the Tradition & Renewing Evangelicalism: A Primer for Suspicious Protestants"* by D.H. Williams  (Perhaps a little *too basic* for most Celtic Lay Monks – perfect to give to the skeptical!)

## Christian History:

*"Here I Stand: A Life of Martin Luther"* by Roland Bainton

*"Church History in Plain Language"* by Bruce L. Shelley

*"History of the Christian Church,"* Volumes 1-6 by Philip Schaff

*"The Ecclesiastical History of the English People"* by the Venerable Bede (Only the section on the ancient Celtic Monks; Scholarly)

*"The History of the Church: From Christ to Constantine"* by Eusebius (Scholarly)

251

Note: The books directly below are some of my all-time favorite books. I've read them three times each (so far) but I realize that they are not for everyone. *If* you are a Christian who *loves the History of Christian Doctrine and Liturgy,* they are **must read**:

*"Credo"* **by Jaroslav Pelikan** (Scholarly)

*"The Christian Tradition,"* **Volumes 1-5, by Jaroslav Pelikan** (Scholarly)

*"The Shape of the Liturgy"* **by Dom Gregory Dix** (Scholarly)

## Apologetics:

*"I Don't Have Enough Faith to Be an Atheist"* by Norman L. Geisler and Frank Turek

## Excellent Audio Bibles:

*Word of Promise* **(Dramatic Audio Theater:** *New King James Version***)** Old and New Testament (Available separately or together). Read by Innumerable Top Actors and Actresses – listens like a Movie Soundtrack. Thomas Nelson Publishers. Our favorite!

*New Testament* **Read by Johnny Cash** (*New King James Version*).

*Holy Bible* **NIV Read by David Suchet** (Complete Bible: New International Version) (Suchet played: *Hercule Poirot*" in the Television Series).

## Excellent Audio Bible Commentary:

*Thru the Bible Radio:* **Dr. J. Vernon McGee** (Commentary on the Entire Bible) 5-Year Radio Program: listen daily on Christian AM Radio. Available on CD or MP3 at ttb.org I've listened to the entire Commentary at least 6 times and look forward to listening to Dr. McGee off and on for life! Also available in Book form, which we also have (the transcribed Radio talks), for reference use. (www.ttb.org)

S.G. Preston

# *Recommended Ministry:*

## *Redeem TV*  **Streaming Goodness.  Our Favorite TV Channel!**

(Christian Film Streaming Service Founded by Bill Curtis, President of *Vision Video / Christian History Institute*.

"A donor-supported, ad-free, streaming service with no fees.  Our goal is to provide edifying and redemptive visual media content for all ages."

**redeemtv.com      watch.redeemtv.com**

## *Christian History Magazine*  **Our Favorite Magazine!**

Published four times per year, and available by donation through the *Christian History Institute* ministry.  We have subscribed for over a decade and have collected back issues of all but four of the over 125 past issues!

**christianhistoryinstitute.org**

# *Recommended Films:*

**Key:** **(In Bold) Must See.**
(*In Italics*) *Highly Recommended.*

## Full-Length Films:

*"Brother Sun, Sister Moon"* by Franco Zefirelli (early ministry of St. Francis)

*"The Nativity Story"* (Keisha Castle-Hughes)

*"Esther"* (Bible Collection: F. Murray Abraham, Louise Lombard) (Made for TV: 1 Hr.)

*"Luther"* (Joseph Fiennes)

*"St. Patrick: The Irish Legend"* (Patrick Bergin, Malcolm McDowell). Excellent! But some may not like that fictional "Legendary" stories are also included.

*"Hudson Taylor"*

*"The Gospel of John"* (Word for Word: *Good News Bible*) The Film is fantastic! (The additional Commentary at the end is worthless: we recommend not watching it).

## Docudramas:

**"Martin Luther" (PBS)**

*"St. Patrick: Apostle of Ireland"* (includes the complete actual words of St. Patrick)

*"Robber of the Cruel Streets"* (About: George Muller)

## Documentaries:

*"A History of Christian Worship: Ancient Ways, Future Paths"* (6 DVDs)

*"History of Christianity"* (6 Parts on 2 DVDs) by Dr. Timothy George

S.G. Preston

## *Celtic Christian:*

*"My Journey to Life: On the Trail of Celtic Saints"* by Rainer Walde
*"Blessing Europe: The Legacy of the Celtic Saints"* by Rainer Walde

# *Bibliography:*

**Primary Sources**:

Adomnan of Iona, St.; *Life of St. Columba* (Penguin Books, 1995)

à Kempis, Thomas; *The Imitation of Christ* (Random House, 1998)

Athanasius, St.; *On the Incarnation*; (St. Vladimir's Seminary Press, 2003)

Athanasius, St.; *Life of Antony* (Ancient Christian Writer's Series; Paulist Press 1950)

Augustine, St.; *The City of God* (Hendrickson Publishing, 2009)

Augustine, St.; *The Confessions* (Barnes & Noble, 2007)

Augustine, St.; *Epistle to Januarius* (Letter 53, Chapter 2); Fathers; (New Advent, 2020)

Benedict, St.; *The Rule of St. Benedict* (Random House, 1998)

Bede, St.; The Venerable; *The Ecclesiastical History of the English People* (Translated by Leo Sherley-Price; Penguin Books, 1990)

Bede, St., The Venerable; *The Life and Miracles of St. Cuthbert, Bishop of Lindisfarne* (Internet History Sourcebook Project; Fordham University)

Basil the Great, St.; *The Hexameron* (CreateSpace Publishing, 2014)

Basil the Great, St.; *Monastic Rule of St. Basil the Great* (Athletis Publishing, 2018)

Bonhoeffer, Dietrich; *The Cost of Discipleship* (Touchstone, 1995)

Bonhoeffer, Dietrich; *Psalms: The Prayer Book of the Bible* (Augsburg, 1970)

Bounds, E.M.; *Power Through Prayer* (Destiny Image, 2007)

Bounds, E.M.; *The Complete Works of E.M. Bounds On Prayer* (Baker Books, 1990)

Brainerd, David; *The Life and Diary of David Brainerd*; Edited by Jonathan Edwards (Baker Books, 1989)

Brother Lawrence; *The Practice of the Presence of God* (Baker Books, 1989)

S.G. Preston

Cassian, John; *The Conferences* (Translated by Boniface Ramsay, O.P.; Newman Press, 1997)

Cassian, John; *The Institutes* (Translated by Boniface Ramsay, O.P.; Newman Press, 2000)

*Catholic Encyclopedia, The*; Pope Honorius I, Entry by J. Chapman; New York: Robert Appleton Company, 1910)

Climacus, John; *The Ladder of Divine Ascent* (Paulist Press, 1982)

Davies, Oliver; Translator, *Celtic Spirituality* (Paulist Press, 1999)

*Didache, or The Teaching of the Twelve Apostles* (Translated by James A. Kleist, S.J., Ph.D.; Newman Press, 1948)

Eusebius; *The History of the Church: From Christ to Constantine* (Penguin Books, 1989)

Foxe, John; *Foxe's Book of Martyrs* (Bridge-Logos, 2001)

Hippolytus; *On the Apostolic Tradition* (St. Vladimir's Seminary Press, 2001)

Irenaeus of Lyon, St.; *Against Heresies,* Books 1-3 (Paulist Press, 2012)

Josephus, Flavius; *The Life* (CreateSpace, 2013)

Lewis, C.S.; *Mere Christianity* (HarperCollins, 1996)

Lewis, C.S.; *Letters to Malcolm: Chiefly On Prayer* (HarperCollins, 1984)

Luther, Martin; *Luther's Small Catechism* (Concordia, 2017)

Murray, Andrew; *With Christ in the School of Prayer* (Classic Reprint, 2017)

Norris, Kathleen; *Dakota: A Spiritual Geography* (Mariner Books, 2001)

O'Maiden, Uinsean, OCR (Translator, *The Celtic Monk: Rules and Writings of Early Irish Monks* (Cistercian Publications, 1996)

*Oxford English Dictionary* (Oxford University Press, 2012)

Packer, J.I.; *Growing In Christ* (Crossway Books, 2007)

Packer, J.I.; *Knowing God* (InterVarsity Press, 1973)

Palladius, *The Lausiac History* (Ancient Christian Writers Series, No. 34; Paulist Press, 1965)

Patrick of Ireland, St.; *The Works of St. Patrick* (Ancient Christian Writers Series, No. 17; Paulist Press, 1953)

*Service Books of the Orthodox Church* (St. Tikhon's Monastic Press, 2013)

   *The Divine Liturgy of St. Basil the Great*

   *The Divine Liturgy of St. John Chrysostom*

Shakespeare, William; *Romeo & Juliet* (

Spurgeon, Charles; *Spiritual Warfare In A Believer's Life* (YWAM Publishing, 1996)

Spurgeon, Charles; *The Treasury of David*; (Commentary on the Psalms; Updated Edition in Today's Language; Thomas Nelson, 1997)

Tertullian, *The Chaplet, or De Corona* (Lighthouse Publishing, 2015)

Tertullian, *On Prayer* (Kessinger Publishing, 2015)

Thoreau, Henry David; *Walden: or, Life in the Woods* (Houghton Mifflin, 2004)

Tolkien, J.R.R.; *Tree and Leaf* (HarperCollins, 2001)

Torrey, R. A.; *The Power of Prayer* (Zondervan, 1971)

Tozer, A.W.; *The Knowledge of the Holy* (HarperCollins, 1961)

Vincent of Lerins; *The Commonitory of St. Vincent of Lerins*; Paul A. Boer Sr. Editor (Veritatis Splendor Publications, 2012)

## Secondary Sources:

Adam, David; *Fire of the North: The Illustrated life of St. Cuthbert* (SPCK, 1993)

Adam, David; *Flame in My Heart: St. Aidan for Today* (Morehouse Publishing, 1998)

Andreopoulos, Andreas; *The Sign of the Cross: The Gesture, the Mystery, the History* (Paraclete Press, 2006)

Arblaster, Paul D.J.; *Celtic Christianity: Yesterday, Today, and for the Future* (Virtualbookworm.com, 2002)

S.G. Preston

Bitel, Lisa M.; *Isle of the Saints: Monastic Settlement and Christian Community in Early Ireland* (Cornell University Press, 1990)

Bainton, Roland; *Here I Stand; A Life of Martin Luther* (Penguin Books, 1995)

Cahill, Thomas; *How the Irish Saved Civilization* (Doubleday, 1995)

Dix, Dom Gregory; *The Shape of the Liturgy* (Continuum, 1945)

Dorsett, Lyle W.; *E.M. Bounds: Men of Prayer* (Zondervan, 1991)

*Encyclopaedia Britannica* (1911), Vol. 14, Page 789 (Ireland, Church of)

Englebert, Omer; *St. Francis of Assisi: A Biography*; Translated from the French by Eve Marie Cooper (Servant Books, 1979)

Hunter III, George G.; *The Celtic Way of Evangelism: How Christianity Can Reach the West...Again* (Abingdon Press, 2000)

*International Standard Bible Encyclopedia,* 1915; Orr, James, M.A., D.D., General Editor (Entry for: "Hours of Prayer" by Henry E. Dosker)

Moorhouse, Geoffrey; *Sun Dancing: Life in a Medieval Monastery and How Celtic Spirituality Influenced the World* (Harcourt Brace & Company, 1997)

Oden, Thomas; General Editor; *Ancient Christian Doctrine,* Vol. 1-5 (IVP Academic, 2009)

Oden, Thomas, Gen. Ed.; *Ancient Christian Commentary On Scripture,* 29 Volumes (InterVarsity Press, 2005)

Papavassiliou, Vassilios; (Commentary on) Climacus, St. John; *Thirty Steps to Heaven: The Ladder of Divine Ascent for All Walks of Life* (Ancient Faith Publishing, 2014)

Pelikan, Jaroslav; *The Christian Tradition,* Vol. 1-5 (University of Chicago Press, 1971)

Pelikan, Jaroslav; *Credo* (Yale University Press, 2003)

*Philokalia, The*; Vol. 1-4 (Faber and Faber, 1983)

Preston, S.G.; *Answers to Prayer* (PrayerFoundation Press, 2019)

Preston, S.G.; *Prayer as a Celtic Lay Monk* (PrayerFoundation Press, 2018 )

Schaff, Philip; *History of the Christian Church,* Vol. 1-8 (Hendrickson, 2006)

S.G. Preston

# *Index:*

(*Note:* there are no entries for certain words: including *Christ, Holy Spirit, Christianity, Bible,* and *Prayer*; because they are mentioned or implied on nearly every page.)

## A

S.G. Preston

# B

Bach, Johann Sebastian; 63
Bainton, Roland (Author: *Here I Stand: A Life of Martin Luther*); 143
Banff National Park, Canada; 97
Bangkok, Thailand; 23
Baptism, Baptized; 39 , 209, 210, 231, 241
Baptists; 18, 147, 169, 172
Barbarians (Goths, Visigoths, Huns, Vandals); 76, 226
Barrows, Cliff; 10
Basil the Great, St.; 65, 66, 134, 225, 222, 223, 226, 231, 235
Basilica of St. Francis (Assisi, Italy); 25, 30
Bede, The Venerable, St.; 24, 33, 135, 206
Beehive-shaped Stone Huts; 32
Bells; 55, 61
Benedict of Nursia, St.; 135, 226, 243, 244
Benedictine Monks; 227
Berlin, Germany; 226
Bernard of Clairvaux, St.; 135
Bessenecker, Scott; 40
Bethlehem, Israel; 57
Bible School (Francke); 155
Big Ben, London, England; 201
Billy Graham; (see: Graham, Billy)
*Billy Graham Evangelistic Association*; 10, 11
Biographies, Christian; 132
Bishops of the *Communion of Evangelical Episcopal Churches*; 21
Bitterroot Valley, Montana; 96
Blacksmith Mike (Made Monk Bob's Bell); 61
Bob's Bell (Lay Monk Bob); 52, 61
Bodybuilding (Weightlifting); 186, 187
Bohemia (Moravians); 154
Bonhoeffer, Dietrich; 35, 36, 37
Bonhoeffer, Karl-Friedrick (Brother of Dietrich); 37
*Book of Common Prayer*; 14, 107
Books, Christian; 116
Booth, William & Catherine (Co-Founders, Salvation Army); 135
Born Again Protestant Monks; 25, 29, 38
Boston, Massachusetts; 31

# C

# D

S.G. Preston

DVDs, Christian; 11, 18

E

Early Church; 34, 35, 39, 63, 65, 88, 89, 114, 134, 135, 146, 235
Early Church Era; 135
Easter; 57, 58, 83
Eastern Orthodox; 13, 54, 57, 58, 78, 81, 89, 101, 110, 132, 203, 207, 208,
    225, 231, 235
    Greek Orthodox, 18, 19, 21, 54
    Greek Orthodox Archdiocese of America; 19, 21
    Hieromonk Kyrill (Theotokos Hermitage); 13, 110
    New Skete (Eastern Orthodox), 18, 21
    Orthodox Monks; 56
    Orthodox Nuns; 59
    Russian Orthodox; 13, 54
    Russian Orthodox Chandelier; 54
Eastern Roman Empire; 76, 220
*Ecclesiastical History of the English Nation* by Bede; 24
*Echinades*; 224
Ecology, Patron St. of (St. Francis); 43
Ecuador (Missionary Martyr Jim Elliott); 157
Ecumenical Patriarch of Constantinople (Great Schism); 208
Edo Period (Japan); 52
Edwards, Jonathan; 135, 139, 150, 151, 156, 157
Egypt; 49, 67, 68, 69, 95, 112, 134, 197, 205, 210, 213, 215, 216, 218 ,
    219, 220, 222
Elijah; 132, 213
Elliott, Jim (Missionary Martyr, Ecuador); 157
*E.M. Bounds: Man of Prayer by* Lyle W Dorsett; 163
England (English); 24, 153, 155, 172, 191, 195, 197, 199, 201, 208
English Baptist (Spurgeon); 169, 172
*English Standard Version* Bible (ESV): 56
Ephesus (Apostle John, Bishop of); 89
Episcopalians; 134
*Epistle to Januarius* (His Son) by St. Augustine; 237
    "When in Rome..." (Ambrose); 237
Equator; 63
*Eremites, Eremitic* (Hermit Monks); 219, 220

S.G. Preston

Holy Land; 220
Holy Nativity of the Theotokos Hermitage; 13
Holy Roman Emperor Charles V (Luther); 142
Holy Roman Emperor Henry II (Filioque); 207
Holy Scriptures (see: Scriptures, Holy)
Holy Table; 54
Holy Week; 58
Honoratus of Lerins, St. (Gaul/France); 243
Horizon Christian High School; 20
Hospice; 166
Hours of Prayer (see: Prayer, Hours of)
Huaorani (Auca) Indians of Ecuador (Jim Elliott); 157
*Hudson Taylor* (Film); 180
*Hudson Taylor's Spiritual Secret* by Dr. and Mrs. Howard Taylor; 180
Humility; 215
Hungary; 240
Huns; 76
Hus, Jan (John Huss); 135, 152, 156
Hymns; 61, 112, 113, 117

I

Idaho; 96
Idol, Idolatrous; 243
Illinois; 13, 17, 40, 60, 95
*Imitation of Christ, The*; by Thomas à Kempis; 44
Incarnation; 212
Incense; 54, 55, 56
Independent Anglican Communion; 20
Independent Christian Reformed Evangelical; 18
India; 10, 130, 155, 157
Intercession (Prayer); 121, 123, 174
Intercessor, Christ our; 93, 129
Internet; 106
*In the beginning...* (Boston Globe Article); 38
iPods; 41
Ireland; 17, 18, 19, 20, 25, 28, 31, 32, 33, 42, 75, 135, 170, 244
Irenaeus of Lyon; 16, 134, 203, 204
    *Against Heresies* by Irenaeus (*Rule of Faith*); 17, 203, 204

273

## J

## K

S.G. Preston

# L

# N

Nara, Japan (Visiting); 52
Nash, Leah (World-class Photographer); iii, 38
National Parks; 70, 97
Native Americans; 139, 149, 156, 159
Nativity Fast (Eastern Orthodox Advent); 57
Nazis; 36, 226, 227
Near East; 56, 63, 69
Neo-Platonism; 216
New Covenant; 87
*New Friars, The* by Scott Bessenecker; 40
New Guinea, Papua; 12
*New International Version*; ii
New Jersey (David Brainerd); 149, 156
New Mexico; 70
New Monasticism; 18, 37, 40, 41, 42, 43, 46, 77, 88, 153, 210, 223
New Monasticism (Dietrich Bonhoeffer); 37
New Monasticism, the Original (Old Monasticism); 201, 244
*New Monasticism: What It Has to Say to Today's Church* by Jonathan
    Wilson-Hartgrove; 41
New Park Street Chapel, London (Spurgeon); 172
New Skete (Eastern Orthodox); 18, 21
New Testament; 35, 73, 75, 83, 114, 132, 142, 152, 155, 204, 220, 245
Newton, John; 44, 135, 136
New York State; 149
Nicene Creed; 67, 68, 87, 91, 202, 203, 205, 206, 207, 208
*Nine Affirmations, The*; 64, 86, 111
Nine Ways to Pray; 121
Ninian of Caledonia, St. (Scotland); 33, 75, 135, 243
Nitschman, John (Moravian Missionary); 156
North Africa; 69, 77, 230
North America; 32, 39, 106, 139, 149, 159
North Carolina; 11, 20, 38
Northern England; 24
Northern Ireland;
North Pacific Current; 52
Northern Ireland; 20
Notre Dame Cathedral, Paris;

Nova Scotia, Canada; 18
Novice Monks (Thomas à Kempis); 44
Nursia, Italy (St. Benedict); 226, 243, 244

# O

Ohio;
Oil Lamps; 51, 54
Old Covenant; 87
Old Monasticism (Dietrich Bonhoeffer); 37
Old Testament; 45, 132, 153, 155, 213, 220, 245
Olive Oil; 54, 59
Omnipotence; 212
Omnipresence; 211
Omniscience; 211
One Solitary Life (Can Change the World); 245
*On Prayer* by Tertullian; 114
Ontario, Canada; 130
*On the Incarnation* by St. Athanasius; 69, 217
Open Brethren Movement (Founder: George Müller); 182
Open Heart Surgery; 28
*Operation Auca*, (Jim Elliott, Huaorani Tribe, Ecuador); 157
Oratory (Chapel); 243
Orphanages, Christian (Francke, Müller); 155, 179, 182, 191, 195
Orders, Monastic: 69, 228, 244
    *Augustinians*; 39, 44, 138, 154, 226, 229
    *Benedictines*; 227
    *Brethren of the Common Life*;
    *Carmelites* (Brother Lawrence); 146
    *Friars Minor, Order of* (Franciscans); 13, 30, 214, 232, 244
        *Order of St. Clare*; 244
        *Third Order* (SFO, Secular Franciscan Order); 244
    *Knights of Prayer Lay Monks*™; 15, 26, 114
    *Lollards* (Preaching Order); 153
    *Servei Dei* (*Servants of God*; Founder: St. Augustine); 229
    Women's Monastic Communities; 220, 244
Orders, Preaching; 244
Ordinary Time; 58
Oregon; 14, 50, 52, 53, 157

S.G. Preston

Roman Army Cavalry Officer (Marin of Tours); 240
Roman Britain (St. Patrick); 32
Roman Catholic; 17, 43, 51, 57, 58, 61, 78, 89, 107, 108, 110, 133, 203, 206, 208, 208, 230, 235
Roman Cavalry Officer (Martin of Tours); 240
Roman Citizen; 220
Roman Emperors; 68, 90, 118, 210, 217, 234, 236
Roman Empire; 76, 77, 217, 226, 240
Rome, Fall of (476 A.D.); 226
Rome, Italy; 29, 76, 207, 208, 234, 237
Rome, When in... (Ambrose); 237
*Romeo and Juliet* (Act II, Scene II) by William Shakespeare; 133, 171
*Rule of Faith,* (Apostles, Athanasius); 203
Rule, Monastic; 221, 225, 226
  *Rule of St. Basil the Great* (*Long Rule* and *Short Rule*); 75, 225
  *Rule of St. Benedict*; 226
  *Rule of St. Pachomius*; 75, 221
Russian Orthodox; 13, 54
Russian Orthodox Chandelier; 54
Ryle, J.C. (Evangelical Anglican Bishop); 134, 135, 172

# S

Sacrifice, Morning (Temple); 202
Saint-Honorat Island, Monastery on (Lerins Islands, France); 243
Sapporo, Japan; 52
Samson of Wales, St.; 33, 135
Sanctuary; 54, 98, 126
Sanctuary Lamp; 59
San Francisco, California; 15, 31
San Luis Potosi, León Guanajuato, Mexico; 31
*Sayings of the Desert Fathers* (See: Desert Fathers)
Schaeffer, Edith; 136, 152, 170, 171, 182
Schaeffer, Francis; 136, 170, 171, 182
Scotland; 18, 75, 162, 243
Scot; 17
*Scriptural Knowledge Institution* (Founder: George Müller); 191
Scripture, Meditation on; 86, 104, 105, 121, 126, 127, 129, 149, 198

S.G. Preston

# V

Vancouver, Washington; *Title Page*, iii, 20, 26, 39, 42, 50
Vandals; 76
Van Steenwyk, Mark; 43
Vatican II; 58
Vermont; 23
Vincent of Lerins, St. *("What is believed everywhere... ")*; 14
Virgin Mary *(Nicene Creed)*; 209
Virginia; 19
Visigoths; 76, 242
*Vision Video*; 11, 116 , 151, 253

# W

*Walden* by Henry David Thoreau; 69
Wartburg Castle (Luther Hidden); 143
Washington (State); iii, 20, 26, 39, 42, 50, 94
Webpages (See: *Prayer Foundation, The*)
Weightlifting (Bodybuilding); 186, 187
Wesley, Charles; 156
Wesley, John; 44, 135, 151, 156, 162, 164
Westminster Chimes;
West Virginia; 14
Western Advent; 57
Western Church; 58, 230, 235
Western Europe; 76, 221, 242
Western Roman Empire; 76, 220, 226
Westminster Chimes; 201
Whitefield, George; 135, 151, 156
Whithorn Monastery, Caledonia/Scotland (Founded by St. Ninian); 243
Wilberforce, William; 135, 136, 137, 156
Willow Creek Community Church, Illinois; 40
Wilson-Hartgrove, Jonathan; 41
Wisconsin; 95
*With Christ in the School of Prayer* by Andrew Murray; 129, 136
Wittenburg Cathedral; 74, 143, 154
Women's First Monastic Community (Egypt); 220
World Missions Era (1800's); 135, 152